The Small Business

Legal

Guide

2nd Edition

The Critical Legal Matters
Affecting Your Business

Lynne Ann Frasier, Esq.

LEARNING RESOURCES CENTER

 Sourcebooks, Inc.
Naperville, IL

Rpl. copy
7-01

#38010747

Published by Sourcebooks, Inc.
P.O. Box 4410, Naperville, Illinois 60567-4410
(630) 961-3900
FAX: (630) 961-2168

Editorial: Todd Stocke
Cover Design: Scott Theisen
Interior Design and Production: Scott Theisen, Sourcebooks, Inc.

This publication is designed to provide accurate and authoritative information in regard to the subject matter covered. It is sold with the understanding that the publisher is not engaged in rendering legal, accounting, or other professional service. If legal advice or other expert assistance is required, the services of a competent professional person should be sought.

From a Declaration of Principles Jointly Adopted by a Committee of the American Bar Association and a Committee of Publishers and Associations

Library of Congress Cataloging-in-Publication Data

Frasier, Lynne Ann.
    The small business legal guide : the critical legal matters affecting your business / Lynne Ann Frasier.—2nd ed.
       p. cm.
    ISBN 1-57071-216-6
    1. Small Business—Law and legislation—United States—Popular works. I. Title.
KF1659.Z9S574   1998
658.02'2—dc21   97-50070
                                                CIP

Printed and bound in the United States of America.
VHG Paperback — 10 9 8 7 6 5 4 3

Dedication

To my husband, B. Roland Frasier, III, Esq. (my partner in life and in law) for teaching me that two people can share a common bond of strength, loyalty, and conviction of a true and loving relationship; and

To my furry and feathery "kids," Napa, Sonoma, Casper, Timon, and Misty, for their endless love and affection; and

To my mom, Jane Maraschiello, my dad, the late Anthony Maraschiello, my sister, Debbie James, and my brother, Tony Maraschiello, for believing in me from the beginning.

Contents

Part II: Planning Your Business

Part III: Operating the Business

Part IV: Franchising

Part V: The Four Keys to a Successful Business

Entrepreneurial Assessment Questionnaire Comparison

Forms 1.1-1.6 Corporate Bylaws, Resolutions, Meeting Minutes

Form 2 IRS Form 2553: Election of Subchapter S Status with Instructions

Form 3 Articles of Organization of California Limited Liability Company

Form 4 UCC-1 Standard Financing Statement

Form 5 UCC-3 Request for Information or Copies

Form 6 Sale of Assets Agreement

Form 7 Sale of Stock Agreement

Form 8 Fictitious Business Name Statement

Form 9 State Name Reservation

Form 10 IRS Form SS-4: Federal Employer Identification Number

Form 11 IRS Form SS-8: Independent Contractor Factors

Form 12 IRS Form W-4

Form 13 INS Form I-9: Employment Eligibility Verification

Preface

Everyone dreams. Some people dream of owning their own business; others dream of reading an entertaining business book. *The Small Business Legal Guide* aims to be one of the few business book to carry out both dreams. It'll be entertaining so you'll read beyond the first chapter, and by doing so, you'll learn four keys necessary to unlock the door to your dream business. Many people leave in their imaginations what they could very successfully attain in real life. Why? Because they lack knowledge of handling legal issues and dealing with government agencies.

That's true no matter what experience they bring to the table. I remember when my partner and I first opened our law firm. Each of us brought to the partnership valuable knowledge from prior experience. My partner, who is now my husband, had negotiated multimillion dollar deals and I had experience in appraising a variety of businesses. Yet, I remember when we decided to open the firm. We understood that the firm had to comply with administrative regulations and federal, state, and local laws. But which ones? There were so many questions to ask and so many procedures to follow that we almost became overwhelmed. But like many others, we had the American dream to be entrepreneurs.

The fact that you're reading this book means you can identify with the courage and excitement which drove us to our venture. We followed our dream and opened our firm and have been assisting business owners ever since. Now its your turn; don't let anything stop you, but pursue it wisely.

Introduction

So you want to get into business on your own. Are you CRAZY? Haven't you heard the statistics? Don't you know the odds are against you? Just ask your friends. Most will be more than happy to tell you that you will be eaten up by the economy or by competitors who are already established in business. What do you mean you don't care? Have you really considered the pros and cons?

Okay, you convinced me that you are serious because you chose to pick up this book instead of some juicy love story. So what are you waiting for? Let's get started. If you are getting into business, you may as well be armed with knowledge which will enhance your chances of being successful from the start. That's right, from the start. The odds are, if you read this book, you will use the four keys necessary to be successful in your own business.

The Small Business Legal Guide is designed to assist you, the entrepreneur, to carry out your dream of owning a business. It is the *first book* which will assist you in starting, purchasing, or operating a business using simple procedures and complete legal agreements, as well as provide entertainment, interactive stories, and mini-tests along the way. This book should be used as a guide in forming and managing a small business. It is not intended to render legal, accounting, or other professional advice. However, it is clearly written and discusses the business climate in general, and each of the subjects discussed in this book can assist the small business owner.

This book is divided into five parts. Part 1 is designed to help you focus on the formation of your business, whether you plan to start from scratch or by purchase. Chapter 1 discusses the various forms of operating a business, from the Sole Proprietor to the Limited Liability Company and more, and the advantages and disadvantages of each. Chapter 2 discusses purchasing an existing business, addressing it from the purchaser's point of view. Then you can take a mini-test regarding liability issues that can affect your business entity.

Part 2 will help you see the whole picture of your business by explaining the often invisible plans and details you will need right from the start. By addressing the issues in this section, you will avoid a whole world of problems that may hamper you down the road—from losing your business's name to losing your business altogether.

Searching for and reserving a name for your business are the focus of Chapter 3, pointing you in the direction of filing Fictitious Business Name Statements, and incorporation and trademark offices. Chapter 4 will put you in touch with essential government agencies, most notably the Internal Revenue Service—before they get in touch with you. Chapter 5 debates working at home versus renting commercial space. It will also help you sharpen your negotiation skills for setting up that all-important lease, and includes a mini-test to discuss lease negotiation.

Then, Chapter 6 breaks down the essential issues of employment. It first offers a mini-test to discuss the difference between an employee and independent contractor and the ramifications of each. The crucial details involved in simply having and keeping employees is covered, and lastly, Chapter 6 discusses trade secrets and insurance.

Part 3 is designed to help you do the one thing you must learn in order to stay in business—protect your backside. In handling ongoing operations, Chapter 7 discusses tax matters, from state to federal. Chapter 8 will show you how not to sign your life away by thoroughly addressing the obligations and dangers involved in contracts. It also presents a mini-test to get you thinking legally and introduces you to the contract boilerplate and what the boilerplate clauses mean.

As the final section in Part 3, Chapter 9 discusses intellectual property, including copyrights, trademarks, trade names, patents, licensing, and protecting your intellectual property against counterfeiting. And if you not sure how GATT, NAFTA, and other international laws affect your intellectual property, this chapter will help clear up the issues. Again mini-tests are given to assist you in actively learning about each type of intellectual property.

Part 4 aims you in the direction of the successful entrepreneur by encouraging your business vision. The dos and don'ts of franchising are addressed to give you sight of what you and your business can achieve. Chapter 10 can help guide you to the right franchise sources and get you to ask the right questions of a potential franchisor. Chapter 11 delves more deeply into the legal aspects of franchising, including the formation of a Disclosure Document and a Franchise Agreement.

Part 5 will revisit the four keys to a successful business and explain each in more detail to help get you on your way.

The Appendix includes legal agreements, government forms, and telephone numbers of government agencies in the 50 states.

By following the recommendations in this book, you will be able to form your own business entity, purchase an existing business or franchise operation, and comply with statutory laws and administrative regulations so as to save time, eliminate confusion, and avoid unnecessary and costly penalties.

The advantages of owning a business are plentiful. It allows flexibility of time and enables the business owner to realize his or her dream and maximize his or her potential. *The Small Business Legal Guide* is intended to be useful to the business owner who wants to save costs. A business owner well versed in government and legal knowledge, as well as the entrepreneur who has limited knowledge of government and legal issues, will find this book helpful. Anyone can use this book as a management tool to form the appropriate business entity and as a research tool to keep the business from incurring penalties for failure to adhere to laws, rules, regulations, and licensing procedures.

Keep in mind that this book is intended to handle less complicated transactions, and the forms and agreements in the Appendix are intended for instructional purposes or simple transactions only. If legal advice or other expert assistance is required, you should seek the services of competent professionals. Although much care has been taken to insure the accuracy and adaptability of the materials in this book, the author assumes no liability to any party for loss or damage caused by errors or omissions contained in this book, whether such errors or omissions are the result of negligence or otherwise. Additionally, the author makes no warranty that the suggestions and forms are suitable for all business circumstances.

Before getting started with Chapter 1, you may want to complete the following Entrepreneur's Assessment Questionnaire. If you do not take the time to peruse it now, then come back to it, because it may provide insight of what to expect in the entrepreneurial world.

Entrepreneurial Assessment Questionnaire

Please answer the following questions, then compare your answers to the comments in the Appendix (pages 127-130) to see how you compare with successful entrepreneurs:

Are you willing to invest a substantial portion of your net worth in the venture, including taking out a second mortgage on your house if necessary?

_____

_____

What major sacrifices have you made in your lifestyle, family circumstances, and your standard of living to make progress in a previous situation?

_____

_____

Are you driven internally by a strong desire to compete? Please explain.

_____

_____

Would you like to outperform against your previous results or against a competitor?

_____

_____

Do you have a need to achieve? Please explain.

_____

_____

Do you set goals? Please explain.

_____

_____

Have you ever willingly placed yourself in a situation where you were personally responsible for the success or failure of an operation? If so, please state the circumstances.

_____

_____

Are you intimidated by certain people or situations?

_____

_____

Do you have a sense of humor?

_____

_____

Do you have a need to know how you are performing? Please explain.

_____

_____

Do you like constant change or would you prefer a routine?

_____

_____

Are you thinking about retirement? Please explain.

_____

_____

Are you a gambler or would you parachute out of an airplane? Please explain.

_____

_____

Are you driven by a thirst for achievement or a thirst for status and power?

_____

_____

On a scale of 1-10, with 10 being the highest, how reliable are you? Please explain.

_____

_____

On a scale of 1-10, with 10 being the highest, how much integrity do you have? Please explain.

_____

_____

Do you have an urgent need to make decisions immediately? Please explain.

_____

_____

Are you a visionary or would you rather stick with the facts at hand?

_____

_____

In the past, how have you used failure as a way of learning? Please explain.

_____

_____

Do you have high energy? Please explain.

_____

_____

How is your health?

_____

_____

Do you watch what you eat and drink?

_____

_____

Do you exercise on a regular basis?

_____

_____

Do you get away when you know you need some relaxation?

_____

_____

Would you consider yourself creative? If so, please state how.

_____

_____

Do you believe you have high intelligence and conceptual abilities? Please explain.

_____

_____

Do you inspire others? Please explain.

_____

_____

Do you like to figure out how things work? Please explain.

_____

_____

Do others tell you that you do things differently than most? Do you believe them?

_____

_____

Part 1

Starting Your Own Business from Scratch or by Purchase

So you weighed the advantages and disadvantages of getting into business and now you have decided to do it. Now what? Suddenly, you find yourself noticing all types of businesses. That's right, the same corner market that has been there for years, the toy store you used to ride your bike to, and perhaps, your favorite Italian restaurant. You may have seen these businesses before, but you never focused on them until now. Now you find yourself wondering whether they are a proprietorship, partnership, or corporation. Well, this is the first key for a successful a business: *you have to focus on formation,* i.e., the form of business in which to operate.

This part will provide information on the following formation topics:

- The most common forms for operating a business.
- The advantages and disadvantages of each type of business form.
- Purchasing an ongoing business from the purchaser's point of view.
- Evaluating the prospective business.
- Determining if perfected security interests exist in assets being purchased.
- Determining if bulk transfer laws are applicable.

After reading this part you will have the knowledge necessary to form your own business from scratch or purchase an existing business, and you will understand the best form that suits your present needs.

Chapter 1

The Most Common Business Entities

Sole Proprietorship

The sole proprietorship is the simplest form in which to do business. It is not a legal entity by itself. It is nothing more than the alter ego of a natural person, which means that a natural person directly owns the business and solely enjoys the profits. Unfortunately, it also means that the person is also directly responsible for its liabilities and debts. In the United States, the sole proprietorship is the most popular way of starting a new business. However, once created and maintained in a successful manner, many proprietorships are switched to partnership or corporate status when the appropriate time arises.

Formation

No legal filing is required to form a sole proprietorship.

Advantages of the Sole Proprietorship

- **Formation costs are low.** A proprietor opens a bank account with a minimum amount. If a proprietor needs capital to get started, he or she can use personal charge cards and loan the company the amount of purchases that are needed.

- **No government requirements.** With one exception, a sole proprietorship is not required to file any legal documents with a government agency. The exception is that if the business name does not reflect the owner's surname or if it implies additional owners, then most states will require a proprietorship to file a Fictitious Business Name Statement.
- **Autonomy.** A sole proprietor has the sole right to manage the business as he or she sees fit.
- **Tax benefits.** Profits are passed directly to a sole proprietor without the double taxation that occurs in the corporate structure. Losses are beneficial if a proprietor needs a write-off for reducing the amount of taxes that he or she must pay.
- **Freely transferable interest.** A proprietor can very easily transfer or sell the sole proprietorship to any person or entity.

Disadvantages of the Sole Proprietorship

- **Personal liability if assets are insufficient.** Since a proprietorship is not a separate legal entity from its owner, the owner runs the risk of personal liability if the business is sued and the business assets are insufficient to cover the claim. Even where the proprietor does not own personal assets at the time of forming the sole proprietorship, if later on, he or she acquires personal assets, the new assets may be subject to business creditors' claims.
- **Personal liability for mistakes of employees or agents.** The proprietor is personally liable when an employee or agent acts in a negligent manner during the course of his or her agency or employment. Some proprietors obtain insurance to protect themselves against this type of negligence. However, insurance may be insufficient to meet some or all the claims, and even if sufficient, insurance may be wiped out after one catastrophic event.
- **Duration is limited.** A sole proprietorship is dissolved by death or bankruptcy of the proprietor. This is a grave

position for a nonowner spouse who is employed in the business at the time the owner spouse dies or is declared bankrupt. The non-owner spouse is simply left out in the cold without a business.

General Partnership

When two or more people join together to make a profit, a general partnership is formed. Most of the time a general partnership is treated as the alter ego of its partners, which means the partnership is nothing more than the partners acting separately or as a collective legal entity. However, the partnership may be treated as a separate legal entity under three different scenarios: 1) a partnership can hold and convey real property in its own name; 2) a partnership can sue or be sued in its own name rather than in the name of the partners; and 3) in bankruptcy procedures, the partnership is considered separate from its owners and thus, if a partner files bankruptcy, the partnership is unaffected and vice versa.

Formation

No legal filing is necessary to form a general partnership. However, it is a good idea to have a Partnership Agreement drafted, because without one, state law prevails and the agreement created by your state may not be what you had in mind.

Advantages of the General Partnership

- **Formation costs can be low.** A partnership can generally open a bank account with whatever minimum deposit it takes to open the account.
- **No government requirements.** With few exceptions, partners are not required to file any legal documents with a government agency to form a general partnership. One exception is when the partnership name does not show the owners' surnames or if it implies additional owners. Then, state law may require that the partnership file and publish a Fictitious Business Name Statement.

- **Equal right to management and control.** Each partner has an equal right to participate in management actions.
- **Tax benefits.** Profits earned by the partnership are passed directly to the partners without double taxation that occurs in corporations. Losses are passed directly to general partners. This may be beneficial for a partner who needs a tax write-off.

Disadvantages of the General Partnership

- **Personal liability.** Partners risk personal liability if the partnership is sued and the partnership assets are insufficient to cover the claim. To make matters worse, general partners are "jointly and severally" liable, which means a business creditor can satisfy his claim from all or any partner. So, if one partner is wealthy and owns a considerable amount of personal assets and the others do not, the wealthier partner risks losing it all. This is true even if the other partner was the cause of the claim.
- **Personal liability for mistakes of employees or agents.** All partners are personally liable when an employee or agent acts in a negligent manner during the course of employment or agency. This means if an employee runs an errand for you on company time, and causes an automobile accident, you may be personally liable to the unfortunate third person who was involved in the accident. It also means if an employee trips over a typewriter cord and the typewriter falls on his foot, not only may you be without his services for the length of time that it takes to heal his broken foot, but you may also be personally liable if his condition leads to another injury.
- **Duration is limited.** Unless otherwise agreed upon in the Partnership Agreement, the partnership is dissolved by death or bankruptcy of a partner. Thus, one partner may be left hanging if the partnership is dissolved in the middle of a promising transaction.
- **Any partner can bind the partnership.** Each partner is an agent of the partnership. Therefore, the partnership is bound and liable for debts incurred by a partner if the

third party could have reasonably conceived that the acting partner was apparently carrying on partnership business.

- **Tax to partners.** Partnership income is taxed to the partners at their level of individual income. This is true even in situations where the income is not distributed to them.

- **Equal right to management and control.** If a conflict arises between partners and deadlock results, management decisions and action come to an abrupt halt. It is a good idea to include a clause in your Partnership Agreement that dictates a course of action which the partners will follow in the event the partners disagree on a management decision. Not only may this circumvent a crisis later on, more importantly, it will show each partner how the other will handle problems before they occur.

- **Transferability of interest is restricted.** Unless otherwise agreed, no one can become a new partner without the consent of all the existing partners. This may stifle growth of the partnership. It may also cause dissension between existing partners if one partner wants to transfer his or her interest and the other will not consent.

Limited Partnership

A limited partnership comprises one or more general partners and one or more limited partners. Limited partnerships are typically created because a general partner needs investors, and limited partners need an investment which allows them to share in profits or take income tax deductions for losses at minimum risks.

Formation

The limited partnership is generally formed when a Certificate of Limited Partnership is filed with the appropriate state government office, which is generally the Secretary of State or Department of Corporations.

Advantages of the Limited Partnership

- **Limited liability of limited partners.** The limited partner enjoys limited liability in excess of his investment so long as the partner does not partake in management affairs.
- **Limited partner's interest is freely transferable.** Unless the Limited Partnership Agreement states otherwise, a limited partner can freely transfer his or her right to receive profits in the partnership to any person or entity.

Disadvantages of the Limited Partnership

- **Government filing requirements.** The general partner must file a Certificate of Limited Partnership with the appropriate government office. Until the certificate is filed, the partnership is treated as a general partnership, therefore exposing all limited partners to personal liability.
- **Formation costs can be expensive.** Setting up a limited partnership is generally more costly than a corporation.
- **Duration is limited.** Death or incapacity of a limited partner has no effect on the partnership status.

General Corporation

A general corporation is a separate legal entity, apart from its owners. The owners are called shareholders because they hold shares of stock in the corporation. The shareholders elect directors, who are responsible for managing the affairs of the corporation. If more than one director is elected, the corporation has a board of directors. The directors oversee operations of the corporation and either elect or appoint officers to carry out the day-to-day functions. The officers usually comprise a president, secretary, and treasurer, and sometimes one or more vice presidents. Of course in many small corporations, one person may hold all of the above positions.

Formation

The corporation is typically created when the Articles of Incorporation (Articles) are filed with the office of the Secretary of State or Department of Corporations. The Articles are a legal document which lists essential information about the corporation. Typically, Articles state the corporate name, corporate purpose, number of shares authorized, name and address of the initial corporate agent, and the principal place of business.

Forms: Bylaws, Resolutions, and Corporate Meeting Minutes

Form Number 1.1 in the form section of the Appendix at the back of this book is an example of a set of corporate bylaws (rules by which a corporation is governed); Form Number 1.2 is an example of a joint resolution of the board of directors and shareholders; Form Number 1.3 is an example of a waiver of notice to hold a board of directors' meeting; Form Number 1.4 is an example of what board of directors' meeting minutes may look like; Form Number 1.5 is an example of a waiver of notice to hold a shareholders' meeting; Form Number 1.6 is an example of what shareholders' meeting minutes may look like.

Generally, under the laws of every state, each corporation is required to conduct annual meetings of directors and shareholders. These meetings and their proper documentation are important for many reasons, including protecting shareholders from personal liability as a result of piercing the corporate veil and protecting corporate directors, officers, and shareholders from personal liability to past, present, and future creditors and tax agencies. The forms referenced in this section can be used as guidelines in preparing your own corporate forms. Generally, the directors are elected at the annual meetings of shareholders and the officers are elected at the annual board of directors' meetings, as the Appendix forms indicate.

Advantages of the General Corporation

- **Limited liability.** As a separate legal entity, the corporation is solely responsible for its debts and liabilities. Therefore, if a claim from a business creditor is in excess of the assets of the corporation, the creditor cannot attach the personal assets of the shareholders. However, limited liability protection for shareholders can be lost if corporate formalities are not followed. To avoid such liability, corporations need to follow at least the following two formalities: hold annual meetings for shareholders and directors, and not commingle corporate funds and assets with personal funds and assets.

- **Easier to obtain financing.** Banks and venture capitalists will provide financing more easily to a corporation than to a sole proprietorship or partnership.
- **Stable appearance.** Whether it is true or not, many customers, suppliers, and bankers believe corporations are more stable than sole proprietorships or partnerships.
- **Shareholder's interest is freely transferable.** Unless there is a restriction on the transfer of stock, shareholders are free to transfer their ownership interest in the corporation.
- **Perpetual existence.** As a separate legal entity, a corporation enjoys perpetual existence.

Disadvantages of the General Corporation

- **Government formalities must be followed.** Typically, government instructions for preparing corporate documents are either nonexistent or sketchy. The novice incorporator may incorrectly prepare Articles of Incorporation or he or she may not include needed information in the documents. Furthermore, when issuing stock, the corporation must either comply with registration requirements of securities laws or qualify for a security exemption. If the corporation fails to comply with one or the other, it may incur liability when government securities agencies track down the corporation.
- **Costs are greater upon formation.** Filing and tax fees must be paid upon formation. This is the most cited reason to avoid conducting business in the corporate form.

- **Annual meetings and corporate formalities.** Shareholders and the board of directors must hold annual meetings and the corporation must comply with other formalities so as not to lose its separate corporate identity. Failure to follow these formalities may result in personal liability to shareholders, directors, and/or officers of the corporation.
- **Double taxation.** A corporation must pay taxes at the corporate level when it declares a dividend or distribution to shareholders, and shareholders must pay taxes at their individual tax levels when they receive the dividend or distribution.

Subchapter "S" Corporation

A general corporation that elects "S" status is a general corporation which, in effect, is taxed like a partnership. The general corporation must qualify as a small business before it can elect "S" status. A small business qualifies under the federal regulations if it meets all of the following requirements: 1) it has 75 or less shareholders; 2) it does not have any corporation, partnership, or nonresident alien as a shareholder; 3) it issues only one class of stock (Sometimes the IRS will treat shareholder loans as a second class of stock. Therefore, one must be very cautious when preparing loan documents.); and 4) it is an eligible domestic corporation.

Formation

Once it is determined that the corporation can qualify, the business owners elect "S" status by filing the proper documents with the Internal Revenue Service and state taxing authority. To elect "S" status on the federal level, obtain IRS Form 2553 from any IRS office, follow the instructions provided with the form, and file the form with the Internal Revenue Service at the address listed on the form for your particular state. There is no additional fee for electing "S" status with the IRS.

Form: IRS Form 2553: Election of "S" Status

Form Number 2 in the form section of the Appendix is a copy of IRS Form 2553, used to federally elect "S" status. You can use the mentioned form (including instructions) to make your federal election of "S" status. To make a state "S" election, contact your state taxing authority and ask for the form used to make the state election.

Advantages of the "S" Corporation

- **Centralized management, limited liability, continuity of existence.** By virtue of its corporate status, the "S" Corporation reaps the same benefits as a general corporation, like centralized management, limited liability, and continuity of existence.
- **Avoids double taxation.** Profits and losses "pass through" to the shareholders, and therefore, "S" corporations avoid double taxation.
- **Profits are taxed at individual shareholder rates.** Under the current rate structure, where taxable income exceeds approximately $100,000, the corporation will pay greater taxes than the individual. Thus, in "S" corporations generating over approximately $100,000, income may be passed through to the shareholders at their lower rates.

Disadvantages of the "S" Corporation

- **Complex tax laws.** Because of their complexity, the IRS allocates a whole section of the tax code to deal exclusively with "S" Corporations, and those who are not well acquainted with the code risk losing the election because they fail to meet certain terms.
- **Calendar year-end requirement.** Businesses electing "S" status today are typically required to have a calendar year-end absent a strong business purpose for a fiscal year.
- **Shareholders are restricted.** Corporations or partnerships cannot be shareholders.

Limited Liability Company (LLC)

Currently 46 states have enacted legislation to create Limited Liability Companies (LLCs). LLCs are attractive business entities for entrepreneurial businesses, investment partnerships, venture capital projects, high technology and development businesses, and other small or medium-sized businesses. (A few states have also enacted Limited Liability Partnerships. Call your state offices if you want further information on this new business form.)

Formation

LLCs are formed when the Articles of Organization are filed with the Secretary of State and the members of the LLC execute an Operating Agreement.

Form: Articles of Organization

Form Number 3 in the form section of the Appendix is an example of the document used to form a Limited Liability Company in California. Forms for other states can be obtained by contacting your state of interest. The Operating Agreement is a complex document and must be drafted on a case-by-case basis.

Advantages of the LLC

More advantageous than a Limited Partnership or an "S" Corporation. In a limited partnership, at least one of the general partners is liable for the debts of the partnership, whereas in an LLC, all members may be protected from such liability under certain circumstances. Additionally, participation in management affairs in an LLC will not result in loss of limited liability protection, which is the case if limited partners get too involved in management decisions in a limited partnership. An LLC is more flexible than an "S" Corporation, in that the LLC does not require only one class of stock, nor does it limit the number of shareholders to 75.

Flexibility in structuring entity. Many states offer broad flexibility in structuring the LLC by allowing the Operating Agreement to overrule default provisions that would otherwise govern the entity. This flexibility makes the LLC attractive for both passive investment and actively managed businesses. Thus, the LLC would be an ideal vehicle for passive investments because the LLC (via the Operating Agreement) may permit the entity to be run centrally by a limited number of members or managers. On the other hand, it would be an ideal vehicle for actively managed businesses because the Operating Agreement may provide for active participation of all members.

Disadvantages of the LLC

Not the most beneficial entity for larger companies. The LLC may not be the best entity choice for larger public companies because there may be a restriction on issuing membership interests (like restrictions on issuing stock in corporations). Under various state laws, some LLCs cannot be perpetual and certain types of businesses may not qualify.

Chapter 2

Purchasing an Existing Business

Finding Opportunities

Consider the following factors when deciding whether a business is right for you:

- The industry you're currently involved in.
- The industries you have skills and experience in and your temperament.
- Whether you're truly interested in doing the type of work for a lifetime.
- Whether you know enough about the business.
- How much money you have to invest.
- What kind of financial backing you need and can get.

There are several sources to look for a business opportunity. Some are listed below:

Trade Sources. Contact suppliers, distributors, manufacturers, trade associations, and even trade schools to ask about businesses that are for sale.

Professionals. Ask attorneys, accountants, bankers, and consultants. They'll often know who's selling a business.

Yellow page listings under Business Brokers. Look here, but keep in mind that this may not be the best place to look for three reasons: 1) the broker's commission usually depends on the price of the business; 2) the listed businesses are well-known in the industry; and 3) there's no real financial evaluation done in determining its fair market value, because most brokers use a ratio which may or may not give a reliable account of the actual value of the business.

Evaluating the Prospective Business

The term "caveat emptor"(buyer beware) truly applies when purchasing a business. Unfortunately, as many purchasers can attest, the process of negotiating and completing the purchase of a business is scary enough without being haunted afterwards by additional debts to pay because the deal was not what you thought. A purchaser new to the entrepreneurial world, as well as a veteran, should at least follow the following procedures:

Determine the seller's motivation for selling. Ask yourself what is the seller's real motivation for selling the business. The oral reasons may not be the truth. Especially look for issues relating to health, retirement, moving out of state, obsolete products, government condemnation, expiring lease, problem with creditors, and inability to expand. You need to dig deeper to find out why the seller really wants to sell.

Get industry statistics. Get historical data from the Chamber of Commerce and trade associations and read the data. This information should provide statistics about fatality start-ups and industry averages. You should take this information and compare it with figures obtained from financial statements and profit ratios of your prospective company.

Look at the financial condition of the company. Do a spreadsheet analysis of the last five years of financial statements and federal tax returns. (If the business has been around that long. If not, look at as many years as the business has been in existence.) Check for any patterns or perks, and at the least, consider balance sheets, income statements, and an array of other issues.

Balance Sheet Analysis

Assets:

Cash Account. See if any excess cash is listed on the balance sheet. If so, adjust the cash account downward and make an adjustment on your spreadsheet. Make sure working capital is the amount required to successfully operate the business. It's not necessarily the amount that's listed on the balance sheet. You need to investigate how much is needed.

Accounts Receivable. Check to see when accounts receivable are generally paid. Is it thirty, sixty, or ninety days, or perhaps beyond six months? Determine the percentages for each length of time. On your spreadsheet analysis, don't include any amount that's over 45 days late because after that time the accounts are generally uncollectible. Also, look to see who is collecting. Is it the seller or does a collection agency handle the accounts? Consider whether a stricter policy should be established to alleviate some excess in the receivables?

Inventory. How much inventory is included? Is it in good condition? What items are slow moving? Which are obsolete? What is the turnover rate? If much of the inventory is old or unsaleable, you need to make an adjustment on your spreadsheet to reduce the worth of the inventory.

Equipment, Furniture, Fixtures. Are these assets adequate? Are machinery and equipment a large part of the sale? If so, you should get an appraisal of them. Is the equipment what you really want?

Building and Land. Does the business qualify under existing zoning regulations? If land is included in the business deal, get an appraisal because the seller may have it listed on the balance sheet for one value and it may be worth another amount.

Intellectual Property. Does the business own a trademark, service mark, copyright, or patent? If so, will they be included in the sale? If not, will you be able to obtain a license to use them? Make sure your spreadsheet reflects the value of the intellectual property if it's going to be included in the sale.

Customer Lists. Are names and addresses included in the sale? If so, how well developed are they? Figure a percentage of losing some of these contacts.

Business Reputation. Does the business have a reputation? If so, is it good or bad? How long has it been established? Has it always operated out of the same location? If not, how many years in each location? How satisfied are the clients or customers? You should get a list and contact some of them at the appropriate time.

Covenant Not to Compete and Goodwill. How much of the purchase price is going toward a Covenant Not to Compete and Goodwill of the business? Does this seem reasonable? What are you really getting for each?

Liabilities:

Accounts Payable. Are any accounts past due? If so, do those creditors have any liens against the assets that you want to purchase? You'll need to run a UCC-3 search to determine if the assets are free and clear. (You'll know how to do this by the end of this chapter.)

Notes Payable. Will any notes to the sellers have to be paid with the proceeds of the sale?

Income Statement Analysis

Income:

Sales. See if sales are consistent during the five years (or number of years that the business existed). See if unusual perks or nonrecurring income exists. Question all abnormalities.

Expenses:

Rent. If business property is owned and rent is being paid, make sure the rent equals what's currently being paid by an arms-length transaction. If the rent is not at fair market value, make an adjustment on your spreadsheet and substitute in a reasonable rent. If the business is renting property, how long is the lease? Ask for a copy and read the terms to see if there will be a problem with the seller assigning the lease to you. Are there options to renew upon expiration? Is the lease transferable when it expires?

Salary. If the owner's salary appears unusual for the industry, contact the trade association to find out a reasonable salary and make an adjustment on your spreadsheet to substitute in the reasonable trade industry amount.

Travel Expenses. If travel expenses are extraordinary, adjust them downward on your spreadsheet.

Perks. Look at the amenities and perks, like money for a spouse's car, or a luxury car, boat, club dues, or excess conventions. Find anything that you, as the purchaser, wouldn't be interested in buying and delete them on your spreadsheet and make sure they're not part of the sale.

Miscellaneous Issues to Consider

Suppliers. How many suppliers does the company have? Is there a variety or only a few suppliers?

Location. Is the neighborhood or the building deteriorating? Does the area have sufficient traffic? Does the area bring in the base of its clientele? Is parking adequate and convenient? Is the business capable of putting up a sign? After reviewing the financials, look to see how much the business is really worth to you. If the records reflect a financial loss, determine the reasons and make sure you consider if and how you can turn it around. If the seller isn't willing to provide this financial information, you should think twice about purchasing this particular business.

Do perfected security interests exist? If you're going to purchase a business, you must understand what "perfecting a security interest" means, and you must know how the following four terms relate to each other: debtor, security interest, secured party, and collateral. A "debtor" is a person who has incurred a debt. If the debtor grants to the person to whom the debt is owed, interest in certain property to secure the debt, the interest is called a "security interest." The person to whom the secured debt is owed is known as a "secured party." The property in which the security interest is held is called "collateral."

What does it mean to perfect the security interest and how is it done? Perfecting a security interest means the secured party can keep the collateral if the debtor fails to make payments. Generally, one perfects a security interest either by filing a financing statement, which is the most popular method of perfection, or by taking possession of the collateral. To perfect a security interest by filing a financing statement, the secured party obtains a "Form UCC-1—Standard Financing Statement" from any legal stationery store. He or she fills out the form as instructed and lists the equipment or assets that will be protected, then the debtor signs the form and the secured party files it with the appropriate government agency, which is either the Secretary of State or County Recorder, depending on the type of assets to be protected. Once the UCC-1 form is filed, the secured party's interest is perfected, which means the secured party has priority over the property.

If you are about to purchase a business with equipment and assets, or if you are just going to purchase all or substantially all assets of a business, you need to search the records of the Secretary of State and/or County Recorder to determine if the equipment or assets are free and clear. To make such a search, you will need to obtain Form UCC-3—Request for Information or Copies from any legal stationery store. After you've prepared it according to the instructions on the form, you'll need to file it, along with a nominal fee, with the proper government agency, which handles the collateral subject to your particular transaction. This search will determine if the assets or equipment are tied up by someone else.

Forms: UCC-1 and UCC-3

Form Number 4 in the form section of the Appendix is a sample Form UCC-1—Standard Financing Statement. Form Number 5 is a sample Form UCC-3—Request for Information or Copies. Do not use these forms, as each state requires it own format. Instead, obtain both forms from any legal stationery store in your area.

If you find a perfected security interest. If you find a perfected security interest before you purchase a business or assets of a business, you have the option to do one of the following: 1) get out of the transaction; 2) make the sale contingent upon the seller obtaining a release, termination, or subordination of the prior interest; or 3) proceed with the transaction, with a reduction in the purchase price because of the additional risk involved.

Is compliance with bulk transfer laws required? Many people incorrectly believe the seller has the burden to comply with bulk transfer laws, but that is not true. The purchaser has the responsibility to comply when the situation warrants compliance. Therefore, it is incumbent for the purchaser to know when he or she must comply.

Three situations where the purchaser must comply with bulk transfer laws include: 1) when the seller transfers a substantial part of his inventory, merchandise, equipment, and supplies, and the transfer was not in the ordinary course of business; 2) if the business being purchased is in the business of selling or manufacturing merchandise; and 3) if the business being purchased is a restaurant, bakery, or cafe. One situation where the purchaser does not have to comply with bulk transfer laws is where the business being sold only sells merchandise as an incidental means of providing a service. For example, a consulting firm, law firm, medical firm, accounting firm, travel agency, or hair salon would not be subject to bulk transfer laws.

How to comply with bulk transfer laws. To comply with bulk transfer laws, the purchaser must complete the following steps: 1) prepare a notice to creditors of the bulk transfer (generally must be at least 12 business days before the sale is to be consummated); 2) record the bulk transfer notice at the County Recorder in each county where the property is located; 3) publish the notice at least once in a newspaper of general circulation in the county where the property is located, and in the county where the seller's principal place of business is located; and 4) notify the County Tax Collector in each county where the property is located.

Why comply with bulk transfer laws? If bulk transfer procedures are not done properly, unsecured creditors can attach any assets transferred as if they still belonged to the seller.

Determine if taxes have been paid. An unsuspecting and unknowing purchaser may be subject to tax liabilities if the seller has failed to pay sales and use tax and unemployment and income tax withholding. To prevent being subject to these liabilities, the purchaser should make sure all sales and use taxes and employment taxes have been paid and he or she should condition the sale of the business upon proof of payment. He or she should also insist upon an indemnity provision in the Purchase Agreement to cover the situation if the tax is imposed.

Sale of Assets

The asset sale is the most common form of selling a business, and several types of assets are typically involved in the sale. Such assets typically include: 1) Real estate, including land, improvements, and fixtures; 2) Equipment, including machinery, office equipment, computer hardware and software, automobiles, and trucks; 3) Furniture, including desks, chairs, reception room furniture, art, plants, etc.; 4) Records, including tax records, financial records, customer lists, supplier lists, bank accounts, bank lists, mailing lists, contracts, leases, files, clients, etc.; and, 5) Intellectual property, including goodwill, patents, copyrights, exclusive contracts, consulting agreements, and covenants not to compete.

Form: Sale of Assets Agreement

Form Number 6 in the form section of the Appendix is an example of a Sale of Assets Agreement, which you can use as a guideline in preparing your own Sale of Assets Agreement.

Sale of Stock

The stock sale occurs when the entire business is sold, which includes assets and liabilities. Liabilities include all liabilities—current and future. In a Sale of Stock Agreement, the seller usually makes representations and warranties about liabilities. The purchaser obtains legal assurances that the corporation is in the same condition as represented and warranted by the seller. The purchaser should also insist on an indemnity provision in case a warranty or representation ends up being other than as stated.

Form: Sale of Stock Agreement

Form Number 7 in the form section of the Appendix is an example of a Stock Sale Agreement, which can be used as a guideline in preparing your own of Stock Sale Agreement.

Sale of Assets Attributes	Sale of Stock Attributes
Sale must allocate a portion of the purchase price to various assets sold. This is what determines the tax consequences of the sale.	An easier way of acquiring a business, if the seller has a small number of stockholders.
More complicated because it requires transferring deeds, assigning leases and contracts, preparing individual bills of sale for assets being transferred and sometimes, complying with bulk transfer laws.	Usually handled in a shorter time frame than a Sale of Assets, and it avoids detailed paperwork because it's not essential to physically transfer assets and rights of the seller.
If the sale involves tangible personal property, it may result in sales tax being assessed, if taxing authorities determine the sale is not an occasional sale. Since only the assets are sold and not the entire business, the purchaser will be responsible only for debts and liabilities which he specifically assumes. (Except by law, certain liabilities will be the responsibility of the purchaser, even if he did not expressly assume them.)	Main disadvantage to the seller is if purchaser has the right to offset (if seller is receiving compensation) from purchaser, who has the right to reduce the payments due if a loss occurs or unexpected liabilities from past operations come up. Main disadvantage to the purchaser is hidden liabilities which may be forced on him. The debt of the corporation is usually included, but the debt may be at lower rates than what would be available at the time the stock sale is made.

Documents Used When Purchasing a Business

Mini-Test Regarding Entity Liability Issues

Let's look at entity liability issues, because you need to take into consideration such issues before you decide which entity best suits your business needs.

Questions

1. You are a sole proprietor in the insurance business. If an employee fails to write up an insurance policy for an insured who has paid his premium over six months ago, are you liable if the insured sues you over a lost damage claim?

2. You and your brother are partners in a pizza restaurant. One of your employees makes a pizza delivery on company time and causes an automobile accident injuring two people. The injured sue you, the partnership, for $100,000. The business is worth only $10,000. Will you be personally liable?

3. On a handshake, you and your friend decide to form a partnership to buy a video arcade. You are going to run the arcade and he is going to repair the machines. You get sick so your partner runs the arcade. A salesman pays him a visit and talks him into purchasing $50,000 worth of antiquated video games. The business has no money and cannot make the payments on the video games. Are you personally liable?

4. You are one of three directors of a corporation, and while you are out of town, the other two directors hold a board meeting to pay stock options to the directors, even though it would dilute the value of the stock and harm the corporation. The shareholders sue for breach of the directors' fiduciary duty to the corporation. Are you liable?

5. You own 80% of the issued and outstanding stock of a corporation and two others own 10% each. You are approached by a corporate looter who offers you a sweet deal to sell your stock at an astronomical price. But you believe the looter's intentions are to harm the corporation by taking its products off the market. You sell your stock to the looter anyway. Are you liable to the minority shareholders?

Answers

1. A proprietorship is not a separate legal entity from its owner. Therefore, the proprietor runs the risk of personal liability if the business is sued and the business assets are insufficient to cover the claim. In this case, the proprietor would be liable.

2. Partners are personally liable for mistakes of employees when employees act in a negligent manner during the course of employment. Therefore, in this scenario, it is very possible that you could be liable.

3. Each partner has apparent authority to bind the Partnership. Therefore, it appears that the Partnership is bound to making the payments, and if it cannot do so, each partner can be held liable for the full amount.

4. Directors who are absent from board of director's meetings where misconduct occurred are not liable for board action. Therefore, under this scenario, you would not be liable. However, if you were habitually absent, you may be liable for a breach of your director's duty of care.

5. Traditionally, shareholders of a corporation have not had a duty to other shareholders. The modern trend is that majority shareholders have a fiduciary duty to refrain from taking undue advantage of or oppressing minority shareholders. So, you could be liable for not allowing minority shareholders to get in on the deal.

Planning Your Business

Consider this scenario. You've searched everywhere—the car, the kitchen, and every nook and cranny in your bedroom. You are late for an appointment, so you finally give in and walk downstairs and ask your spouse, "Have you seen my sunglasses anywhere? I can't find them." A smile comes over your spouse's face, "You mean the ones that are on top of your head?" You reach up and feel your sunglasses. You smile sheepishly because you were concentrating so hard on other matters that you failed to be aware of the obvious.

Well, that is the second key to a successful business: *seeing the whole picture.* Every business owner must deal with certain tasks and activities, whether they are visible to the owner or not. In this part, we will discuss the critical details that help make up the whole picture, including:

- Searching for and reserving a name for your business.
- Contacting essential government agencies.
- Choosing a business location.
- Determining whether to work alone, hire employees, or hire contractors.
- How to deal with employee related issues.
- How to protect trade secrets and confidential information.
- Why you should check into insurance.

Chapter **3**

Your Business Name

How do you decide on the name of your business? The answer is simple: you either purchase an existing business and continue the name, like Ray Kroc did when he purchased McDonald's® Hamburgers, or you create the perfect name, which sometimes means spending countless hours, like IBM® or Xerox® Corporation did. Whatever the case, you'll conduct business under a certain name known as a trade name. However, whether you may safely use the name depends on what actions you take to protect it. If you haven't already, you need to perform the following steps:

1) Search whether the name is being used by another.
2) Reserve the name for yourself.

Searching for the Name

Conduct a search to see if the name is being used by another business. After all, if you think the name's perfect, why shouldn't someone else think so? You may be surprised to find others have come up with the very same name, and you don't have to be in the same industry to confuse the public. For example, I know of a client who operated a chicken restaurant but resisted protecting their catchy name by filing a Fictitious Business Name Statement, incorporating, and/or filing for protection under trademark laws. Sure enough, months later, a pet shop with the same name opened its doors down the street, and soon afterward the restaurant received calls from pet shop patrons inquiring about parrots and other birds. To make matters worse, a national fast food restaurant chain decided to use the same name later on, and obtained protection under federal trademark laws by registering the name with the United States Patent and Trademark Office (PTO). From that day forward, the restaurant owners could not register their name at the federal registry or use it when it came time to expand into other counties. This is because they only acquired common law rights to use the name in the location which existed before the national chain registered the name.

It was only then that the restaurant owners understood the repercussions of not properly protecting their company name. Do not let this happen to you. If you have not already done so, protect your name as soon as you get into business. Make sure it is a name that will be worth spending all your time, money, and effort on; not one which you will spend countless hours litigating over. To determine whether your name is being used by another business, you need to search the following sources:

Telephone Directories. Search for the name in the white and yellow pages of all local telephone directories. Call Information on new listings. Check words that are similarly spelled and words that sound alike but are spelled differently. Chances are if two words are either spelled alike or sound alike, the public may be confused as to the source of the goods or services. You will also be more likely to be involved in litigation over the similarity.

County Recording Office. Search the records in the County Clerk/Recorder's office to see if someone else filed a Fictitious Business Name Statement to conduct business under the same or similar name.

State Incorporating Office. If you're operating as a Sole Proprietorship or Partnership and plan to incorporate in the future, check with the Secretary of State or Department of Corporations to see if your proposed corporate name is taken by another corporation.

Federal and State Trademark Offices. The PTO defines a trade name as anything from a "surname to any name or designation lawfully adopted by persons, associations, corporations, or businesses, which are capable of suing or being sued." Since the gamut of names under this definition could be indefinite, the federal registry does not register trade names. However, if a business uses its name as both a trade name and a trademark, the mark can be registered with the PTO and gain protection under federal trademark laws. Examples of companies that use their marks in conjunction with their name are Coca Cola®, IBM®, and Xerox®. If you're conducting business across state lines, you should conduct a full search of the federal registry, each of the registries in all 50 states, and directories under common law to determine if you can protect your name under federal trademark laws. If you're conducting business intrastate, you should search the records of the state agency that handles state trademarks to determine the availability of protecting your name under state trademark laws.

If you have conducted the above searches, and to your advantage, your company name or a similar name is not being used by another, you can, and should, reserve it for yourself.

Reserving the Name

County Recording Office

There are just four easy steps to filing a Fictitious Business Name Statement. These steps are almost always required in most areas. Your County Clerk/Recorder will let you know if their process deviates from these basic steps:

1) Obtain a blank Statement from the County Clerk/ Recorder or Newspaper of General Circulation and prepare it according to the instructions on the back of the form.
2) File the Statement with the County Clerk/Recorder in the county where the principal place of business exists. Your Recorder will let you know if you need to file with another state agency.
3) Publish your intent to use the name in a Newspaper of General Circulation in the same county where you filed the Statement.
4) Generally, 30 days after publishing, file an Affidavit of Publication with the County Clerk/Recorder.

Once filed, the name is generally protected in the county for five years. Before five years is up, renew by performing the same or similar procedures as outlined for the original filing. Filing a Fictitious Business Name Statement enables you exclusivity of the name in counties where the statement is filed. To protect your name statewide, you should incorporate or seek a trademark.

Form: Fictitious Business Name Statement

Form Number 8 in the form section of the Appendix is an example of a Fictitious Business Name Statement application used in Los Angeles, California. This form is for teaching purposes only. However, each state has a similar form. To protect your name in a county where you are conducting business, simply contact the County Recorder in your state to obtain instructions for filing for such protection.

State Incorporating Office

If you plan to form a corporation, you can reserve a corporate name at the Secretary of State or Department of Corporations. Forming a corporation under your name provides statewide corporate protection of the exclusive use of your name as a corporation. However, incorporating does not protect against trademark infringement. To further protect your name if it is used as a trademark, you must also register it under state or federal trademark laws.

Form: Corporate Name Reservation

Form Number 9 in the form section of the Appendix is an example of a letter written to reserve a corporate name. To reserve a corporate name in your state, simply contact the office of the Secretary of State or Corporation Commission in your state to obtain instructions on whether such a letter is sufficient to reserve the name. If it is not, the agency will usually send you a form, which generally contains the same information as listed in the referenced letter.

Federal or State Trademark Office

If you conduct business intrastate, and your trademark/trade name search of your State Trademark Office reflects that the name is available, you can register the name with the State Trademark Office. If you conduct business across state lines and your trademark search of the U.S. Federal Register, registers in all 50 states, and directories under common law, reflect that the name is available, you can seek registration of the name with the PTO. Remember, however, that corporate names, as such, are not eligible for federal trademark registration. Rather, only corporate names used as trademarks are eligible for registration.

While each case is determined on its own facts, the chances for obtaining trademark registration of a company name may be increased if the following guidelines are used:

1) Use the name of the company with the symbol® if you have registered the mark, or use ™ if you have yet to register it, followed by the generic name of the product or services that the company offers. For example: Apple® Computers or Kelloggs® Corn Flakes.
2) Do not use other trademarks in juxtaposition to the company name.
3) Do not use the company name with phrases like "made by."
4) Do not use the business address in immediate juxtaposition to the company name.

If you have conducted the above searches, and to your chagrin, the same mark exists at the County Office, State Corporate Office, and State or Federal Trademark Office, then other than under common law, you will be unable to protect your name. If you are already in business, you will have the right to use the name at your present location but may be prevented from using it elsewhere or at multiple locations.

If your search of the County Clerk/Recorder's Office proves another has filed a Fictitious Business Name Statement using the name or similar name, then you will be unable to protect your name at the county, but may be entitled to protection if you incorporate or seek protection under trademark laws.

If your search at the Secretary of State or Department of Corporations proves that another has incorporated under the same or similar name, you will be prevented from incorporating under that name, but may be able to file a Fictitious Business Name Statement in the county or obtain trademark protection under state or federal trademark laws.

If your search of the State Trademark Office (if you sell goods or services intrastate) or the Federal Trademark Office (if you sell goods or services across state lines) proves another is using the same or similar name, then you'll be unable to protect your name under trademark laws, but may be able to obtain protection under county name protection or state corporate laws.

A Word of Wisdom

If your search proves that another is using a similar name but not your exact name, you may want to consider abandoning your name rather than seeking protection for it. Why? It's simple. You will spend money seeking protection for it. You will also spend money on stationery, envelopes, brochures, business cards, and perhaps a sign. You will build goodwill under it. Then you may find out that the name is too close to another name and a government agency will not allow your name to be registered. Furthermore, even if the two names can coexist legally, you risk litigation over the similarity because the previous owner may take the position that your name is likely to confuse the public and he or she may sue you over it. Do not let this happen to you. Your name is one of the most important assets of your company. Do not make it a liability. (All marks in this section are registered trademarks or service marks of the respective companies listed.)

Chapter **4**

Contacting Essential Government Agencies

Have you ever stood in line for 45 minutes on a sweltering day in an un-air conditioned building, when the clerk tells you that you are in the wrong line and points to a longer line which has worked its way down around the corner? Perhaps, you gaze from the top of your eyes at the clerk, sigh deeply, glance at the clock, back to the line which just became longer, and walk toward the front door vowing to come back another day—only to forget about it until it's too late and the deadline has passed.

Some say the above scenario describes dealing with the government. Well, sometimes it may, but you need to take care of certain government matters—even if it means ruffling through bureaucratic procedures. This section will make government procedures seem so simple that after reading it, you will offer assistance to your friends in their next encounter with the Internal Revenue Service. Well—maybe you won't go that far. However, you will learn about dealing with the IRS—and don't panic, this contact may not cost you anything.

Internal Revenue Service

Unless you are able to use your social security number for business tax purposes, you must obtain a Federal Employer Identification Number (FEIN) from the IRS. This number is used to identify your business for income tax, payroll, and other federal purposes, and the IRS requires that you apply for the number if you or your business fits one of the following categories:

1) You don't have an FEIN and you will be or currently are:
   a) Paying wages.
   b) Required to use a FEIN on any return, statement, or other document, even if you are not an employer.
   c) Required to withhold taxes on income
2) You'll become the new owner of an existing business, even if the business does not have employees; except that if you will become the new owner by acquiring its stock, then use the FEIN of the corporation.
3) You're forming a partnership or corporation even if it does not have employees.
4) You're incorporating your sole proprietorship or partnership.

Form: IRS SS-4 Federal Employment Identification Number Form

Form Number 10 in the form section of the Appendix is an example of a FEIN application. You can copy this form or obtain an original from any IRS office. The steps involved in preparing this form are listed on the instructions which accompany the form. All you have to do is follow the instructions and file the form with the IRS location listed in the instructions. Once the IRS processes the form, it will send you the nine digit number, which incidentally, is needed before you will be able to establish a bank account, elect Subchapter S status, make a tax deposit, or file a tax return—so file your SS-4 as soon as possible. The good news is there is no fee for filing this IRS form.

State Taxing Authority

You may also be required to obtain a state tax identification number if you will employ one or more persons and the business will pay a stated minimum amount in wages in any calendar quarter. You should contact the state taxing authority in your state to determine whether you need to obtain such a number, and if so, how you go about obtaining it.

Seller's Permit

With limited exceptions, any business that sells tangible personal property must pay sales or use tax. To determine if your business needs to pay this tax, you must first obtain a seller's permit from the appropriate government agency, which is generally the state taxing authority. Check the government pages in the city where you live to determine which state agency to call, and contact that agency to determine which steps to take in order to obtain the seller's permit.

Once you acquire a seller's permit, you will generally have the right to purchase property for resale without paying tax; but, to take advantage of this privilege, you will need to provide a properly signed resale certificate showing your seller's permit number to the vendor. You can usually obtain a resale certificate at any legal stationery store.

The seller's permit is good only for the type of ownership specified and for the address specified. After receiving it, you must notify the appropriate government agency when you move your location, change ownership, or sell your business. Notification is especially important when selling your business, because unless you notify them, you could be held liable for the purchaser's transactions.

Collect and Pay Sales and Use Tax

A retailer must have obtained a seller's permit in order to collect and pay sales or use tax. Sales tax is imposed when the retailer sells tangible personal property at retail in-state, and use tax is imposed on storage, use, or other consumption within the state of tangible personal property which was purchased outside the state. The retailer must file sales and/or use returns and make payments to the appropriate state agency even if the business did not sell any merchandise. If the retailer fails to file and make payments, the state agency may revoke or suspend his or her seller's permit and bring suit to collect delinquent taxes.

City Business License

Regardless of the type of business you choose, your business will generally be required to get a business license from a county or city agency that handles these licenses for businesses operating in their territories. Typically, you must obtain a business license within a few days to a couple of weeks of starting or purchasing your business. If you do not obtain the license within the designated time, you may end up paying a penalty. In rare cases, a license may not be required. Check with your city or county to find out if you do.

Other Government Agencies to Contact

Depending on your type of business, you may need to file for a special license or permit with a certain government agency. Check the federal, state, or local requirements in your area to be sure that you are complying with all laws, rules, and regulations.

Chapter 5

Choosing a Business Location

If you do not purchase an existing business with a set location, you will need to decide whether your business will be located in your home or outside of your home. There are advantages and disadvantages to each. The major advantage of a home-based business is its cost-saving feature, i.e., there is no travel or additional rent expense. The major disadvantages include the residential activities that must go on, such as dogs barking, people mowing their lawns, or kids playing, and that the neighborhood setting may not be impressive to a client or customer as a commercial office setting. The main advantage of renting commercial space is the professional atmosphere and the major disadvantages include additional costs for rent and travel time.

Home-Based Businesses

Many businesses start and are successfully maintained in the home. If you plan to have a home-based business, you will need to consider many issues, but two need your immediate consideration—tax and zoning.

Tax Issues

If you work out of your home, you must take into account possible tax consequences. If you don't have three profitable years in the last five working years, the IRS may allege that you weren't in business, but rather that you were merely enjoying a hobby. If you cannot convince them that you intended to make a profit, you could end up paying a lot more income tax than what you were prepared to pay. However, if you can establish being in business, you can deduct all ordinary and necessary expenses, which include the cost of furniture, equipment, supplies, inventory, etc. Furthermore, you may be allowed to deduct a portion of the "work area" located in your residence, if your residence is used exclusively as a principal place of business on a regular basis.

Zoning Issues

If you plan to work out of your home, you must consider zoning before you get started because it can be quite costly to start a business, and print business cards and stationery with a home address, only to find out that the zoning regulations prohibit businesses in your neighborhood. Before forging ahead in your home-based business, you need to check with the appropriate zoning board in your city to determine if the zoning ordinances preclude you from maintaining a home-based business, or if they will block you from residing in a commercial or industrial zone.

Renting Commercial Space

If you choose to operate a business outside your home, you will find it necessary to negotiate a commercial lease. To enable you to be a savvy lease negotiator, you need to know two basic issues about commercial leases: 1) how leases are generally referred to by persons who deal with them; and 2) how to negotiate one.

How Commercial Leases Are Referred to in the Industry

A commercial lease may be referred to as a gross lease, net lease, triple net lease, or percentage lease. A gross lease means the landlord will

Planning Your Business

assume *all* ancillary obligations under the lease. This includes, but is not limited to, real property taxes, assessments, repairs and maintenance, insurance, and restoration of the property in case of destruction. If *some* obligations are passed to the tenant, the lease is considered a net lease. Sometimes this is also called a modified lease. If all obligations are passed through to the tenant, the lease is called a triple net lease. If the tenant pays a percentage of his or her sales, the lease may be called a percentage lease.

Make sure you understand these differences before you try negotiating a lease. Otherwise, you may end up paying more in expenses than you bargained for and the lease may impose a serious economic hardship on you. You also need to understand that a lease can be for a freestanding building or for a multitenant building. A restaurant owner is more likely to negotiate a freestanding building lease and a retailer or personal service provider is more likely to negotiate a multitenant lease. The landlord or owner of a freestanding building is likely to be more negotiable than one who owns or leases a multitenant building, because the freestanding building is not restricted to fit restrictions from other tenants.

How to Negotiate a Commercial Lease

Many tenants hesitate to negotiate a lease because they think the written words are non-negotiable. As a result, instead of negotiating better terms for themselves, they sign a lease with economic provisions so onerous and one-sided in favor of the landlord that the tenant is forced out of business. Do not let this happen to you because few leases are truly non-negotiable. The fact is that certain clauses may be non-negotiable, but others will be if you work on them. If a landlord offers you a "take it or leave it" situation, strongly consider whether you want to embark upon a situation where the other party is so inflexible.

Deal Points to Consider When Negotiating a Lease

Setoff: If the lease doesn't allow setoff of paying rent if the landlord does not live up to its obligations under the lease, try to amend the lease to provide for setoff so you won't be forced to pay full rent when your building does not warrant it.

Cap on Expenses: Put a cap on all expenses over the term of the lease, otherwise the landlord may increase the rent to an unreasonable amount and you'll be stuck with it.

Utilities: Make sure the landlord is liable if it fails to discontinue or interrupt any utility service. Otherwise, your business could suffer. If your lease doesn't provide for setoff in rent, try to amend the lease to include such setoff and termination if multiple incidents of disruption continue to occur.

Indemnity and Default: Many leases regarding these issues are one-sided in favor of the landlord. If your lease is one-sided, add reciprocal language in favor of you, as the tenant. (Although some states provide coverage for the other party if the lease provides coverage for one.)

Subordination, Attornment: Many leases require the tenant to subordinate and attorn its lease. If your lease requires this, add some language which states you shall only subordinate the lease upon the condition that you receive an adequate nondisturbance agreement from the new parties. This will ensure that your physical possession is not disturbed or that your rent won't be increased if the building is sold.

Non-Competition Clause: Make sure that the landlord agrees not to allow another tenant in the building/shopping center whose primary use is the same as yours.

Personal Guarantees: Many landlords which lease to corporate tenants require their shareholders, directors, or officers to personally guarantee the lease rental obligations. If this applies to you, make sure that you're willing to do this before you sign. Also, if you have to sign a personal guarantee, try to get a cap on your personal liability.

Mini-Test of Your Lease Negotiation Skills

Try your hand at the following situations to see how you'd review the matter:

1. The landlord hands you a lease and tells you that another tenant is looking at the same space so he needs to get it back from you as soon as possible, but no later

than 24 hours. You take the lease home and promise to get back to the landlord the next day. You call your attorney, but he's out of town. You:

[ ] Review the front side of the lease, and if it seems reasonable, make a few changes then sign and return it to the landlord.
[ ] Call the landlord and tell him you can't make a decision yet.
[ ] Sign the lease and return it to the landlord.
[ ] Call the landlord and offer to sign a binding letter of intent until your attorney has a chance to review the lease.

2. You review the terms of a five-year lease for office space which is perfect for your business needs. The minimum monthly rent is affordable, but yearly increases are tied to the consumer price index and you're not sure how much extra you'll have to pay after the first year. You should:

[ ] Counteroffer to pay increases on a fixed basis.
[ ] Agree to pay increases per the consumer price index because the index has not risen much in the last few years.
[ ] Counteroffer to pay no increases.
[ ] Negotiate free rent up-front and pay higher rent in later years.

3. In reading over the lease, you notice you'll be expected to pay your share in common area and operating costs. The office that you're interested in is in one of two buildings located on the same project and the lease doesn't define the common area. Currently, both buildings are 90% occupied. What should you find out?

[ ] Make sure that the current year is considered the base year.
[ ] Make sure the common area is defined to only include your building.

[ ] Make sure that expenses are based on a standard of 90-95% occupancy.
[ ] All of the above.

4. The retail space you're interested in is large enough for your current needs, but you plan on expanding your business in the next few years. You should:

[ ] Request an option on contiguous space.
[ ] Obtain a right of first refusal on all contiguous space.
[ ] Request an option; if that's not possible, a right of first refusal.
[ ] Look for other space.

5. The lease states that you must carry a general liability policy of at least $1,000,000 per single occurrence. You must also carry business interruption insurance and the landlord has the right to require you to increase your insurance limits. Which of these terms should you try to get stricken?

[ ] $1,000,000 coverage per single occurrence and business interruption insurance.
[ ] Landlord's right to require tenant to increase insurance limits.
[ ] Landlord's right to require tenant to increase insurance limits and business interruption insurance requirement.
[ ] All of the above.

Answers to Mini-Test of Your Lease Negotiation Skills

1. Number four is the best choice because it binds you and the landlord into a situation to deal exclusively with each other until you can negotiate the terms of the lease. Number one is insufficient because you have not read the terms on the back. Number two is not good because the other party may rent the space. Number three is obviously not the answer.

2. Number one is the best answer if you can afford the present rent and if the increases are within your estimated budget. Number four sounds good if you need a few months to get started, but be sure that you'll be able to make the payments in later years or you may be trouble. Number three can cause you to lose the landlord's interest and it may not be practical. Number two is not the best answer because past indications may not be a good indicator of future increases and you will not be able to budget for the increases because they are not a fixed amount.

3. Number four includes all the issues that you need to consider and therefore it is the best answer. It is important to make sure that expenses are based on 90-95% occupancy or you'll end up paying more in common area expenses if the building loses tenants.

4. Number three is the best answer because an option is better than a right of first refusal. Number four is not a good answer because you may pay more for less desirable space.

5. Number three is the best answer because standard leases do not usually require business interruption insurance and any clauses to that effect should be stricken. The landlord should also not have the right to require the tenant to increase insurance limits. Number one is not a good answer because most landlords will require a tenant to keep in full force and effect a general liability policy of at least $1,000,000.

Employment, Trade Secrets, and Insurance

Some business owners wear all the hats when they first open their businesses. They act as manager, bookkeeper, and customer service representative all in one. Others hire additional help from the beginning. The main advantage of working alone is the cost-saving feature. The major disadvantage is that tasks may become too difficult for one person to handle, and as a result, the business suffers. The main advantage of hiring others is that your time will be spent on managerial tasks rather than trivial ones. The major disadvantage is the extra costs involved. Before you actually hire someone, you should know the difference between hiring an employee and an independent contractor.

Mini-Test: Employee or Independent Contractor?

If you're going to hire people, you need to know the difference between an employee and an independent contractor. To get a general idea of how close their classifications can be, read the following stories and see if you can determine the worker's correct classification:

1. The worker is a subcontractor who is paid to wire all houses in two different housing developments which are being built by one general contractor. The subcontractor moonlights with another contractor. How should his work with the first general contractor be classified?

[ ] Employee   [ ] Independent Contractor

2. A typist works at a law firm, but sometimes takes work home and on occasion takes on work from two other firms. The law firms have control over the result of the work, but not over the methods of accomplishing the result. The typist should be classified as:

[ ] Employee   [ ] Independent Contractor

3. A worker is in the business of physical therapy. She is hired by a senior physical therapist to work in the senior's office. The worker must abide by office hours, but otherwise is free to schedule appointments as she sees fit. The senior therapist has general power of supervision. The worker should be classified as:

[ ] Employee   [ ] Independent Contractor

4. The subcontractor is paid on a salary basis. His general contractor has the right to terminate the work that the subcontractor is doing, or to change jobs that the subcontractor is working on. The subcontractor should be classified as:

[ ] Employee   [ ] Independent Contractor

5. The salesman receives training from his employer. He works his own hours, but is subject to control and direction of the employer. He works full time for the employer and is paid on a salary basis. The salesman should be classified as:

[ ] Employee   [ ] Independent Contractor

Answers to Mini-Test: Employee or Contractor?

Questions 1 and 3 have attributes more like an independent contractor. Such attributes include the following:

- The worker is in a business separate from the employer who hires him.
- The worker uses his or her own method and generally receives little or no training from the employer.
- Both the employer and worker have the right to terminate the work being done.
- The worker can work for more than one employer at the same time.
- The worker receives payment of a specified sum for a designated result.
- The worker sets his or her own hours.
- The employer has control over the result of the work, but not over the methods of accomplishing the result.
- The employer has general power of supervision, but the worker has full control over details.

Questions 2, 4, and 5 have attributes more like an employee. Such attributes include the following:

- The worker is subject to absolute control and direction of the employer.
- The worker receives training from the employer on how to perform tasks.
- The employer has authority to control work, whether he exercises it or not is immaterial.
- The employer has the right to terminate the work being done, or to discharge the person doing it.
- The worker is paid on an hourly or salary basis.
- The worker works full time for the employer.
- The worker has set hours of work.

If You Hire an Independent Contractor

If you hire an independent contractor, you won't have to pay social security tax, federal or state unemployment tax, or worker's compensation. The independent contractor will pay his or her own self-employment tax and the employer will be relieved from withholding income and payroll taxes. This is very favorable for most employers, and for this reason, the IRS scrutinizes independent contractor relationships very carefully to determine if the relationship should be reclassified as an employer-employee relationship. To deter misclassifying an employee as an independent contractor, the IRS requires business owners to file IRS Form 1099 for each independent contractor who makes a minimum designated amount or more in the tax year. If the business owner fails to issue and file this form, he may be subject to penalties and interest, as well as possible back payments on payroll taxes which would have been paid, had the worker been classified as an employee. (See the Appendix to find out where to obtain IRS Form-1099 Misc.)

Form: IRS Form SS-8: Independent Contractor Factors

The IRS uses 20 factors to determine whether a worker is an employee or independent contractor. These factors can be found on IRS Form SS-8, shown as Form Number 11 in the Appendix. You can use this form or you can obtain Form SS-8 from any IRS office. A brief description of the 20 factors are listed below. If you are contemplating hiring independent contractors, you should peruse this form before doing so. You should also contact the state taxing authority and worker's compensation board in your state because they use factors of their own and you should consider their factors before hiring anyone.

The 20 IRS Factors

Factor 1: Control

This is the single most important factor the IRS considers in determining whether a worker is an independent contractor or employee. If the company has the right to tell a worker how to do the work, it is more like an employment relationship. The IRS has said that all the company needs is to have the right to control; it does not matter if the company does not actually exercise that control.

Factor 2: Training

The IRS believes that the contractor should possess the skills necessary for the tasks. Therefore, if training is necessary, the relationship looks more like an employment relationship. This is because training indicates that the company is not just concerned with the end result, but is also concerned with the means and method of obtaining the result. Training differs from the first factor, control, because training addresses the worker's need for training and control addresses the company's right to instruct.

Factor 3: Integration in Company's Business

If the worker is essential to bringing the company's products or services to market, the relationship is more like that of an employment relationship. If the worker does not perform tasks normally performed by employees, the worker may be a contractor. If the worker's services are essential, the company should try to assert the position that the contractor's expertise is needed to allow the company to perform other necessary functions.

Factor 4: Personal Services

Employees are not allowed to delegate their responsibilities to others unless the employer allows such delegation. Therefore, if possible, the company should allow contractors to delegate their services to their employees or subcontractors.

Factor 5: Hiring and Supervising

It is important not to allow contractors to supervise employees or be supervised by employees. Contractors should not be lumped together with employees, nor should their records be grouped together.

Factor 6: Continuing Relationship

It is best to have contractors work and be paid on a flat-rate basis, rather than on an hourly or salary basis. A contractor should work on one project at a time. A company that changes a contractor's work orders in the middle of a project risks changing that relationship to an employment status. Contractors should not have continued employment and employees should have such an arrangement.

Factor 7: Hours of Work

Generally, if the company dictates a worker's hours, the worker is more likely to be an employee. Within certain guidelines, contractors set their own schedules.

Factor 8: Amount of Time Devoted

Employees are generally required to work full time for one employer. Contractors can and should be encouraged to work simultaneous jobs and not full time for any one job.

Factor 9: Location

It is best if the contractor works out of his or her own location. However, a contractor can be required to work at the company's premises to coordinate with staff or work on computers or equipment located there.

Factor 10: Order of Work

Employees are required to work in the order and sequence that the employer set out. Contractors control the sequence and manner of their own work and the company should not be concerned with anything other than the result.

Factor 11: No Interim Reports

Because the requirement of reports may look like the company is trying to control more than the end result, contractors should not be required to submit such reports.

Factor 12: Method of Payment

Employees are generally paid on an hourly or salary basis. It is best to pay contractors on a flat-fee basis since it is a good link for completed projects.

Factor 13: Expenses

Contractors should always pay their own expenses, pay their own taxes, and share the risks of being in business.

Factor 14: Tools and Equipment

Contractors should own the tools necessary to perform their jobs. However, the investment in such tools varies from industry to industry.

Factor 15: Investment in Own Business

Employees are not required to invest in the company business. Contractors are expected to make such an investment.

Factor 16: Profits and Losses

Contractors should take the risk of loss with the company for nonpayment by customers.

Factor 17: Multiple Companies

Contractors can and should be encouraged to work for multiple companies. Contractors who give up other accounts after working for one company may lose their contractor status.

Factor 18: Public Services

Employees do not perform services directly to the public, whereas contractors advertise and offer their services to the public.

Factor 19: Right to Discharge

Assuming a contractor has a written agreement, the contractor has contractual rights. Under such an arrangement, either party should provide the other with notice to terminate the relationship, or termination should occur after completion of the job. Employees can be terminated at will or they can voluntarily quit at will, whether or not a project is completed.

Factor 20: Right to Quit

Employees can quit at will and contractors should provide notice so as not to look like an at will relationship.

If You Hire an Employee

If you hire an employee, you must pay social security, federal or state unemployment tax, worker's compensation, withholding income, and payroll taxes. However, you'll enjoy the advantage of controlling the employee's time, duties, and way in which the duties are carried out. When you hire the employee, you need to have the employee fill out two government forms: IRS Form W-4 and INS Form I-9.

Form: IRS W-4

Form Number 12 in the Appendix section is a sample of IRS Form W-4. This form should be filled out by each employee on the employee's first day with the company. The information provided by the employee on the form will help to determine the amount of income tax and social security that you need to withhold from the employee's wages. Once filled in, you should keep this form in your personnel records, as there is no need to file the form with the IRS unless requested to do so.

Form: INS I-9 Employment Eligibility Verification

Form Number 13 in the Appendix section is a sample of INS I-9 Employment Eligibility Verification. This form should be filled out by each employee on the employee's first day with the company. Form I-9 in effect states that employers should hire American citizens and aliens who are authorized to work in the United States, rather than aliens who are not authorized to be in the United States. When you hire an employee, furnish this form to that employee and request that he or she fill in the required information and provide you with proof of identification and eligibility to work in the United States. File the completed form in your personnel records and keep it for at least three years, in the event that the Immigration and Naturalization Service requests it.

Critical Employment Issues

As a result of numerous decisions, rulings, and interpretations that are made on a daily basis, federal and state labor laws are constantly changing. With such constant activity, the beginning entrepreneur, as well as the veteran, has trouble keeping abreast of current trends. However, those who do not stay on top of it all may find themselves literally out of business if their business is sued and loses on a wrongful termination, wage claim, or similar unfortunate lawsuit. Do not let this happen to you.

While it is not the purpose of this section to offer specific information on federal and state labor laws (which may overlap), the following issues are frequently litigated and every employer needs to be aware of them.

Interview and Hiring Procedures

Although an employer may require prospective employees to fill out an application, be interviewed, take a written or oral examination, and in certain cases, undergo company paid physicals or background checks, there are limits to what an employer can and cannot do. For example, an employer cannot lawfully inquire about a prospective employee's maiden name, birthplace, religious affiliation, marital and dependent status, general medical condition, physical or mental disabilities, or race. Nor can the employer ask about whether an applicant still owes money on school loans, or whether the applicant has filed any past worker's compensation claims until a job offer is made to the applicant. However, most states allow an employer to inquire whether or not the prospective employee is a nonsmoker or whether he or she is able to perform the functions of the job, as well as require that a photograph be provided, but only after employment begins.

The list of can and cannots is endless, but the entrepreneur must be aware of them. However, each state enforces different regulations; therefore, any employer contemplating hiring employees should check his or her state laws to find out what requirements the business must abide by. To help reduce potential liability for later actions of discrimination or wrongful discharge, employers should use written material during the hiring process. Such material should at least comprise an application and written interview questions, and supervisors and management involved in the hiring process should be required to use these documents at all times.

Exempt vs. Non-Exempt Status

Exempt employees are the business' leaders. They may include administrative, executive, and professional employees, as well as certain commissioned salespersons and others. However, not everyone in the above categories is exempt. Rather, only those who are required to exercise discretion and independent judgment and whose duties reflect the minimum standards required for such exemption are eligible.

Executive exemptions generally include directors and officers of the company. They are the policy makers whose decisions carry a substantial impact on the success of the business. Exempt professionals may include accountants, attorneys, or those engaged in an occupation commonly recognized as a learned or artistic profession, like music, art, acting, and writing. Administrative exemptions may include managers, executive assistants, staff employees, or employees who perform special assignments, and whose primary duties, levels of responsibility, independence of judgment, and required skill are sufficient to meet the standards for the exempt status. All employees in the above categories who do not qualify for exempt status and all other employees are non-exempt.

The most important distinction between the two classifications is that non-exempt employees must be paid overtime wages for hours of overtime worked. To avoid paying overtime wages, employers have been known to pay employees on a salary basis. But, just placing an employee on a salary does not exempt him or her from overtime wage and hour laws. In order for the employee to be truly exempt, he or she must actually perform duties that qualify the position for the exemption. Therefore, before making a decision to exempt any employees, make sure that the employees' actual duties, and not their titles, qualify them for such status. Once an employee is properly classified as exempt, his or her salary should be the same regardless of the number of hours worked.

Making deductions for absentee days, or requiring exempt employees to submit time cards for hours worked, request permission to take partial days off, or make up hours may jeopardize the status of exempt workers. If this status is lost, the employer may be required to pay overtime to all exempt employees. Therefore, employers should avoid the temptation to tie exempt employees to the amount of time that they spend on the job. Instead, employers should pay attention to exempt employees' ongoing value of services which are of consequence to the success of the company.

Employee Contracts, Handbooks, and Policy Manuals

Written contracts, handbooks, and policy manuals serve a variety of useful purposes if drafted properly and kept up-to-date. However, if outdated or if ambiguous language is used, the employer may be subject to a variety of discrimination, wrongful discharge, or other employee-related lawsuits. On the other hand, contracts, handbooks, and manuals that are properly drafted can actually help preserve the nature of certain aspects of the employment relationship. For example, if an employer desires to hire all persons under an "at will" relationship (each are free to terminate the relationship at will), the employer must include clearly understandable "at will" statements in the employment contracts, handbooks, and manuals. If these documents are not consistent, or if the language implies any promises of continued employment, the employer may be liable for a wrongful termination claim should a disgruntled employee be terminated.

Every employer should create an employee handbook, because without one, the employer is significantly more vulnerable to a variety of wrongful discharge lawsuits. The handbook should explicitly and clearly state which employees are covered by the policies written therein, and it should reiterate the "at will" employment relationship, if that is what the employer intended. The handbook should also cover the following topics:

- An introduction describing the purposes of the handbook.
- A policy on the company's commitment to provide equal opportunity and nondiscriminatory practices.
- A wage and hours section describing work schedules, breaks, mealtime, and overtime.

- A benefits section discussing vacation, sick leave, leave of absences, insurance, pension plans, and eligibility requirements.
- A conduct and disciplinary section describing company rules that employees are expected to follow and disciplinary actions for failing to follow such rules.
- An employee acknowledgment and receipt form which the employee must sign showing that he or she agrees to abide by the terms in the handbook.

The policy manual should cover the policies of the company. Again, to adequately help employers, such a manual should be consistent in its terms with the employment contract, handbook, and other written material.

All handbooks and manuals should be carefully drafted and reviewed by management. Then, the employer should submit them to experienced labor counsel for review. The employer who fails to submit these documents to labor counsel because he or she wants to save costs may want to rethink his or her strategy, because the potential liability for outdated or ambiguous language can far outweigh the costs of a review.

Once the contracts, handbooks, and manuals are completed, they should be distributed to management and supervisors, who should be trained regarding them prior to the date that the employees receive them. Similarly, employees should receive the handbooks and manuals in advance of the date upon which the changes or policies will be implemented. Lastly, whenever new material is distributed, the date and names of the persons receiving such material should be well documented and all outdated material should be discarded.

Wage Claims

With few exceptions, employers must pay lawful minimum wages to employees. If they do not, employers may subject themselves to fines or imprisonment or both. The exceptions include hiring minors or persons affected with certain mental or physical disabilities, family members, and sometimes outside salespersons. These exceptions may not apply in every state. Each state has its own criteria for establishing exceptions, so check the laws in your state if you plan to hire employees at less than minimum wage.

If an employer fires an employee, or if an employee voluntarily quits, all final wages earned but unpaid need to be paid within a certain number of days. In California, depending on the circumstances, this is the last day of employment or within 72 hours or less. Check with your state to determine when wages are due and payable. Failure to pay on time could subject your business to penalties, and willful failure to pay in a timely fashion may subject you and your business to further penalties and fines.

Most states also severely limit employers from deducting employees' pay for tardiness, lost tools, and employee debts. Any employer who makes such deductions is risking penalties that are hardly worth the loses that can be incurred. Employers' actions are especially scrutinized when they involve an employee's final paycheck. So, if an employee owes you money or has lost some of your business tools or other items, rather than deduct the amount from his or her paycheck (especially the final one), perhaps it would be better to pay the wages that are due, and file a separate claim against the employee in a small claims or other court proceeding.

If an employer receives court orders to garnish an employee's paycheck, the employer must follow certain rules set out by law. Generally, such rules include not charging the employee for time and costs spent on the garnishment and not discharging the employee because his or her wages are subject to a single garnishment. (However, the employee who is subject to multiple garnishments can be terminated.) If you are asked to garnish an employee's wages, instruction will be provided with the garnishment order. All you need to do is follow the instructions.

Employee Access to Personal Records

Employers are required to keep personnel records for a set period of time which is determined by state law. Employees may inspect and copy all personnel records specified by law. Generally, this includes records that are used to determine the employee's qualifications for employment, promotion, and salary increases. It also includes performance reviews and disciplinary documents.

Documents that employees generally do not have access to include records of criminal investigations and letters of reference. Unless extenuating circumstances exist, employees' inspection rights are limited to a certain number of times per year. If the employer unreasonably denies such access, he or she may be liable for damages to the employee. Furthermore, if a past employer misrepresents a former employee's file or attempts to blackball the former employee from obtaining employment, the employer may not only be liable for damages, but may also be guilty of a misdemeanor. During the inspection, the employer has the right to monitor the inspection to make sure nothing is removed, destroyed, or altered.

Vacation, Holidays, and Leaves of Absence

Vacation and holidays are not required by law. However, if they are offered, they are regulated by law. Within guidelines, the employer can determine the rate that employees accrue vacation or whether they accrue it at all. The employer can also limit how employees take their vacations and whether they must be taken at one time. One thing for certain is that all earned vacation time must be paid when an employee is terminated or voluntarily quits. Vacation is generally earned on a continuous basis rather than on a monthly or yearly basis, which means if an employee is terminated, the employer cannot defer accrual of vacation compensation to the end of the month or year to avoid paying vacation.

By policy, an employee may be required to take all accrued vacation in the year that it is earned. In some states, if the employee does not take the vacation within a certain time period, the employer cannot take it away. However, the employer may install a policy to limit the number of days accrued that cannot be carried over to the next period. In effect this means that before the next time period, the employee will be paid a number of vacation days that equal or exceed the number of days allowed to accrue for the last vacation period. Additionally, an employer may also put a cap on the accrual of additional days until the employee takes some of his or her vacation days. Some employers allow employees to take a paid vacation before the employee earns the time.

Generally, if the employee resigns or is terminated before vacation is earned, the employer is allowed to deduct the wage advance from the final check, so long as the employee was informed in writing before he or she left the company that unearned vacation would be adjusted on the final paycheck. If an employee receives a raise in salary and subsequently quits or is terminated, the employer must pay wages at the rate of pay at the time of separation.

The employer is free to offer or not offer holidays during the year and such offer may be at pay or without pay. Some employers offer a floating holiday. If this holiday is conditioned on a specific event, like the employee's birthday, the holiday will not be considered an accrued vacation day. However, if the employer offers a holiday that is not tied to a specific event, the day is treated like accrued vacation instead of a holiday, and the employer has a duty to pay for the holiday if the employee quits or is terminated and the day was not used.

It is up to the employer's discretion whether or not to offer sick leave. Most employer's who offer sick leave do not allow it to accrue like vacation days, and therefore, the employee can either use it or lose it. Some employers offer a bonus of the number of sick days paid if employees do not use them. To avoid sick leave being lumped with vacation days when an employee quits or is terminated, the employer should be careful not to lump both benefits into a single category.

Leaves of absence for pregnancy, family leaves in certain instances, military leave, and jury duty leave are mandated by law, and the employer must comply with such regulations. Other leaves are by the discretion of the employer. Sometimes employers offer leaves with pay and other times with partial pay or at no pay at all. If the leave is one that is mandated by law, generally the employer must retain an employee's job. However, employers are not usually required to pay salary or benefits either under a mandated or nonmandated leave.

Check federal laws and your state's laws to determine which leaves are mandated and which are exempt from such mandates. If you will employ fifty or more people, make sure to check on the federal Family Care and Medical Leave Act because employees who, at the time this was written, have had at least one year of continuous service, are allowed to take up to 12 weeks in a 12 month period for the employee's own health and family health care matters. Also, make sure to check on the applicable pregnancy leave mandates, because discrimination against pregnant employees is not allowed.

Discrimination and Harassment

So long as the employer does not discriminate against any protected class in the hiring process and during employment, the employer retains the right to select whomever he or she desires for each position available at the company. Protected classes include various classes governed by both federal and state laws. The protected classes under federal law are race, color, religion, sex (including harassment and pregnancy), national origin, ancestry, age (40 and over), mental or physical disability, and those most recently protected by the federal family and medical leave laws. Some state laws will further protect a veteran's status, religious creed, marital status, ancestry, and medical condition. There is also protection for classes of sexual orientation and political activity.

Some discrimination practices are not willful. However, an employer may be liable because of the effect of certain acts that end up being discriminatory. For example, if a prospective employee is interviewed for a position and he or she is covered by a protected class, is qualified for the job, but denied it, and if the employer continues to accept applications, then the applicant may have a case for unlawful discrimination. However, an employer may rebut the discrimination claim by showing that the prospective employee is not being treated any differently than the other applicants or the reasons for different treatment are not discriminatory.

The Americans with Disabilities Act is a federal law that currently applies to all employers of 15 or more employees. It states that employers may not discriminate against any qualified employee who has a disability, but rather the employer must provide reasonable accommodations to assist any worker who has a disability that is covered by law.

The Federal Pregnancy Discrimination Act requires all employers to treat pregnant employees the same as any other employee. Thus, pregnant employees who are unable to work because of childbirth or related medical conditions must be treated the same as any other worker who must take time off because of a disability.

The Federal Age Discrimination Act protects employees who are 40 years or older, engaged in any industry that affects commerce, and are employed by any private company that employs or has employed 20 or more employees for each working day in each of 20 or more calendar weeks in the current or preceding year.

Sexual harassment has received much attention in recent years. According to the United States Equal Employment Opportunity Commission (EEOC), sexual harassment consists of unwelcome sexual advances, requests for sexual favors and other verbal or physical acts of a sexual or sex-based nature when (1) submission to that conduct is made either explicitly or implicitly a term or a condition of an individual's employment; (2) an employment decision is based on an individual's acceptance or rejection of that conduct; or (3) that conduct interferes with an individual's work performance or creates an intimidating, hostile, or offensive working environment. Sexual harassment includes harassment of women by men, of men by women, and same-sex gender-based harassment.

It is impossible to define every action or all words that could be interpreted as sexual harassment. However, the best rule to remember is that harassment is present when one or the other individual indicates that advances, attentions, remarks, or visual displays are unwanted and should be ended. Employers must employ sexual harassment policies that include no retaliation policies and inform their employees of such policies. Failure to institute such policies and to provide an avenue for employees to make reports of such activity may very likely make the employer liable for such actions.

Termination and Employment At Will

Even if an employment relationship is deemed "at will" and the relationship can be terminated by either party at will, an employer may find that his or her right to terminate may be restricted. For example, if the termination violates a contract, company precedent, or specific statute, or if the termination is discriminatory or violates public policy, the employer may find him or herself liable under a wrongful discharge lawsuit.

Employers can attempt to protect themselves against such lawsuits by creating company documents, policies, handbooks, and procedures that show employment is only an at will relationship. Also, managers and supervisors should be instructed not to make oral or written statements to the contrary of the relationship being at will. Such wrongful statements may include representations that the employee will be around as long as the employee performs his or her job in a satisfactory manner. Furthermore, handbooks should not use language that may imply a promise of employment. For example, using the term "probationary" may imply that once the employee has past his or her probation, the employee is guaranteed a position with the company. Therefore, all employers need to draft material, or carefully review their already drafted material, and make sure that all documents do not contain promises or obligations to which employers can be held liable.

If an employer must terminate an employee, it is better if the employer has written work rules to follow. However, these rules should be flexible to allow the employer to take whatever action is necessary on a case-by-case basis. Otherwise, if the rules are too stiff, they may actually work against the employer if he or she does not follow them on a consistent basis. Before a problem gets out of hand, the employer should respond. If an employee is not following the rules or is acting in an inappropriate manner, supervisors should discuss the problem with the employee and such discussions should be placed in the employee's file. If the employee's behavior does not change and if termination is contemplated, make sure the matter is handled by the appropriate persons and again, document what is said.

Employees can be one of the biggest assets of your company. If treated with respect and provided encouragement, they can be your best and most useful ally. If treated poorly, or talked to in a disrespectful or condescending manner, they could be disastrous to your company. You have the choice of how to treat them, and you will either reap the benefits or suffer the pain, so choose wisely.

Protecting Trade Secrets

What is a trade secret? A trade secret is information that derives independent economic value from not being generally known to the public and is subject to reasonable efforts to maintain its secrecy. Trade secrets can be formulas, like the Coca-Cola® formula, patterns, methods and devices, programs, techniques, and compilations. A trade secret gives its owner a competitive advantage over those who do not have access to the secret. It cannot be claimed on something that may be readily available by reverse engineering or disassembly.

What are some examples of trade secrets? Some courts have held that certain customer lists are trade secrets. Other courts have held that employees can send announcements about forming a new business to clients whom they personally served while in the employ of another. However, the employee still owes a duty of diligent and faithful service to the employer during his or her tenure, and therefore, the employee cannot solicit customers before leaving the company. Although, the law is constantly changing regarding the solicitation of customers by former employees, an employer may wish to have a nonsolicitation clause in all Confidentiality Agreements.

An employer may not secure trade secret protection merely by labeling information secret. The information must meet the requirements of what a trade secret can be. All employers should make reasonable efforts to maintain secrecy. They can do so by using confidentiality agreements, informing employees of the existence of trade secrets, limiting access to such secrets on a need-to-know basis, and controlling access to the business and facilities. Employers should have it as their goal to seek protection such that only by improper means could a person access the information.

How Do You Protect against Disclosure by Employees?

Confidentiality Agreements can be prepared to prevent disclosure by current and former employees. Many Confidentiality Agreements contain restrictive clauses known as noncompete clauses. These take the form of an employee's promise that he or she will not engage in certain specified competitive activities, such as soliciting his or her former employer's customers. Generally, these clauses will be enforced if the covenant prevents alienation of a business's long-standing customers or to protect the business from misappropriation or abuse of confidential information.

However, poorly drafted noncompete clauses or ones that are too vague on the time or distance of competing may not pass muster in a court of law. Furthermore, noncompete clauses are generally not enforceable unless the employer can show that the conduct of the former employee is restrainable under unfair competition laws. Also, keep in mind that an employer cannot prevent a former employee from using the general skill, experience, and knowledge that he or she learned on the job. All the employer can do is prevent the former employee from disclosing or using the employer's trade secrets.

One thing that employers can do to attempt to prevent the copying of electronically stored data is to institute exit interview procedures requiring exiting employees to sign a statement saying that they have returned all company information and property. Employers should also send periodic memos to employees stressing the importance of confidentiality and the employees' duties to keep information confidential.

How Do You Protect against Disclosure by Your Company?

Depending on the type of business that you are in, trade secrets can be protected in a number of ways. Employers can use logbooks and require visitor badges or escorts. They can require that visitors sign Confidentiality Agreements and they can have standing nondisclosure agreement clauses in agreements with vendors, consultants, and licensees.

One way to cleverly protect your trade secrets that are in your computer programs is to use intentional typos and place small pieces of erroneous source code in your programs. Lastly, employers should recover all information provided to subcontractors and vendors after their need for it has ended. Employers can color-code sensitive documents and use log in/log out procedures to protect such sensitive documents.

Employers also need to be careful that public disclosures do not jeopardize trade secrets, for example, when the business is on display, or in advertising or publications. If you conduct tours of your business, you should post warning signs where trade secrets could be exposed and the tour guide should give verbal warning to those on the tour. Additionally, anyone taking the tour should be required to write their name on a list. Employers can prevent intentional disclosure by locking files and rooms containing confidential information. Additionally, they can require passwords to get access into the computer system. If necessary, employers can hire security guards.

A very under-used but much needed way to protect trade secrets is to use a shredding machine. Also, avoid or limit telecommunications access. To prevent copying of sensitive documents, such documents should not be kept near copy machines. Plus, requiring the use of a key card to access copiers is almost essential so that only trusted employees have access to the copiers.

How Do You Protect against Disclosure in Litigation?

To prevent disclosure of trade secrets and confidential information in litigation, an employer can claim a privilege, seek in camera rulings on privilege, seek protective orders, and obtain stipulations by the other counsel.

Employee Inventions

Any employer whose industry involves the possible inventions of products and devices, like tools, computer programs, and computer hardware, should have an agreement with his or her employees covering ownership of the inventions. Such agreement should include an assignment of the rights of the invention to the employer. Additionally, the agreement should be prepared and executed at the onset of the employment relationship. Otherwise, the employer may find ownership problems with inventions that are created by employees. The employer is generally not entitled to ownership if the employee invention is:

1) Created on the employee's own time.
2) Created with the employee's own equipment and supplies.
3) Not created through the use of trade secrets belonging to the employer.

4) Not a byproduct of the employer's business or likely to be invented for the employer's business.

5) Not a derivative of any work performed by the employee for the employer.

Having an agreement regarding ownership of inventions can simplify problems which may arise with employee inventions, and thus, employers should always use such agreements.

Insurance

The purpose of this section is to give you an overview of insurance needs. Any savvy business owner will discuss details of specific needs with his or her insurance agent.

General Liability Insurance

A business owner should consider obtaining general liability insurance. This type of insurance covers the situation where a customer slips on the floor and breaks a leg or if an employee runs an errand for his or her employer on company time and causes an accident. It's available as part of an office insurance package.

Health and Life Insurance

If the business owner is the sole breadwinner of a family, he or she may want to obtain life insurance in event of his or her untimely death. Likewise, a partner in a partnership or a shareholder in a corporation may want to obtain insurance on the other partners, shareholders, or key people. Consider obtaining health insurance. One type of health insurance is major medical. This type covers expenses when a person obtains medical services from a doctor, nurse, hospital, etc. Another type is disability income insurance, which covers expenses when the person is disabled.

Mandatory Insurance

If the business has employees, you will need to maintain worker's compensation and state disability insurance. Worker's compensation covers expenses for medical costs, temporary or permanent disabilities, and death benefits. If the business employs only one part-time employee, it generally must have worker's compensation and there are stiff penalties for not providing this type of coverage. State disability insurance covers expenses for an employee who becomes disabled by illness or injury unrelated to employment.

Part **III**

Operating the Business

In the last section we explained the procedures necessary in planning any business. You learned the second key to a successful business: seeing the whole picture. You are now equipped with knowledge that every business owner must consider at some time or another when planning the business. Now, you must consider what every business owner must learn to stay in business. *You must acquire the knowledge necessary to protect your backside.* This is the third key to a successful business. If you protect your backside, you will not have an Internal Revenue Service agent sitting in your living room as you try to explain why you do not owe taxes; you will not enter into a contract from hell; and you will not see your hard-earned inventions or creative work with someone else's name on it without your consent.

After reading this chapter you will know how to protect your backside. You will be able to smile when you greet an IRS agent. You will enter into contracts from heaven, and you will see your work on someone else's product only if you are seeing royalties.

The activities that you must deal with to stay in business are as follows:

- Handle tax matters.
- Enter into economically sound contracts.
- Protect your intellectual property.

Chapter 7

Taxes

Once you have considered the matters involved in planning a business, you must once again think about the Internal Revenue Service (IRS) and handle the following tax matters:

- Estimated Tax.
- Self-Employment Tax.
- If the business has employees: FICA, Withholding, State Disability, Unemployment and Workmen's Compensation.

Tax issues are complex, and an indepth discussion on tax matters is not the purpose of this section. The purpose of this section is to equip the business owner with necessary awareness to handle tax matters.

Federal Estimated Taxes

Regardless of which form of business you choose, be prepared to make estimated income tax payments to the federal government via the IRS. The IRS requires that estimated tax payments for each quarter of the year be equal to one-quarter of ninety percent (90%) of the tax due for the year.

Sole Proprietorships and Partnerships

Sole proprietors and partners use IRS Form 1040-ES to make federal estimated tax payments. The Internal Revenue Service will automatically send Form 1040-ES to a sole proprietor or partner after he or she applies for a Federal Employer Identification Number (see FEIN in Chapter 4). After the individual prepares the form as per the instructions listed on the form, it should be sent with the estimated payments to the IRS at the address listed on the form. These payments are due in four annual installments. The first payment is due on April 15, next June 15, then September 15, and the last one is due on January 15 of the following year. Any remaining federal tax which is not paid by the last payment date in January is due on April 15 of the following year when the individual files his annual tax return. Note: This means that on April 15 of each year, the business owner whose tax year is the calendar year is required to 1) file a tax return for the year ending December 31, and 2) make the first annual installment for his or her estimated taxes of the current year.

Corporations

Corporations are also subject to making federal estimated tax payments. Corporations use IRS Form 1120-W to compute federal estimated tax payments. Corporations make tax deposits by using a federal tax deposit coupon. Both forms are sent to them by the Internal Revenue Service after the corporation applies for and obtains a Federal Employer Identification Number. After computing the federal estimated tax payments on Form 1120-W according to the instructions on the form and filling out the federal tax deposits accordingly, the corporation deposits the amount due on the federal deposit coupons in a bank authorized to accept federal tax deposits.

Note: A stiff penalty may be imposed for failing to make timely deposits directly with an authorized government depository bank. Thus, it is important to receive the coupon book. Any corporation which does not receive this booklet should contact the Internal Revenue Service. Furthermore, a corporation whose coupons are depleted throughout the year should contact the IRS office nearest them. Payments may be due as early as the fourth month of the first year that the corporation exists and will continue on a quarterly basis.

State Estimated Taxes

In addition to federal estimated payments, the business owner should be prepared to make estimated income tax payments to the state government. Check with the appropriate state taxing authority to determine the correct procedures to follow.

Federal Self-Employment Taxes

Self-employment tax to the sole proprietor or partner is the government's way to make him or her pay social security tax. It is required if the sole proprietor or partner makes a profit during the tax year. The corporation does not pay self-employment taxes. Instead, it pays social security tax for its employees. As is the case with estimated taxes, each entity uses a specially designed form suitable for the entity. Contact your nearest Internal Revenue Service office to obtain the correct form.

Sole Proprietorship

A sole proprietor must pay self-employment taxes on any profit derived from the sole proprietorship if his net earnings from self-employment exceed $400. To do this, the sole proprietor will attach Schedule SE to his federal income tax return, i.e., IRS Form 1040. If the sole proprietorship incurs a loss for the tax year, he or she reports the loss on Schedule C of Form 1040.

Partnership

A partner must pay self-employment taxes on his or her share of profits of the partnership. To do this, the partner will attach Schedule SE to his or her individual federal income tax return (IRS Form 1040). If the partnership incurs a loss for the tax year, the partner reports the loss on Schedule E of Form 1040.

Corporation

A corporation does not pay self-employment taxes. Rather, it pays social security taxes for its employees. However, a corporation must report income. It does this by filing corporation federal income tax on IRS Form 1120 (or 1120S if the corporation is a Subchapter "S" Corporation).

State Self-Employment Taxes

Each state also requires the self-employed individual to pay the equivalent of a social security tax. Check with the state taxing authority to obtain further details.

Additional Employer Taxes

The tax matters in this section will be brief. As with other sections on tax, contact the appropriate government agencies or your tax accountant or tax attorney for details.

Social Security and Income Tax Withholding

The most significant taxes that the employer is required to collect are income taxes and social security taxes. If a business owner plans to hire employees, *Circular E, Employers Tax Guide* should be obtained from the IRS. This guide will explain federal income tax withholding and social security tax requirements for employers. Each state also requires an employer to withhold state personal income taxes on wages paid to employees. A business owner should contact the state taxing authority for details.

State Disability, Unemployment, and Worker's Compensation

In addition to state income taxes, a business owner must generally withhold state disability insurance contributions from an employee's wages. He or she must also pay state unemployment tax and worker's compensation insurance. If a business owner plans to hire employees, he or she should contact the state taxing authority.

Chapter

Contracts

As a business owner, you will enter into many contracts. But before you do, you need to be aware of some basic issues in contract law.

What Is a Contract? A contract is an agreement between two or more people where each party promises to do or not to do something in exchange for the other party's promise to do or not to do something.

How Is a Contract Formed?

Make an Offer. One party makes an offer to another party. The person making the offer is called the offeror and the intended receiver is called the offeree. There are times when an offeror's words do not constitute an offer, for example, when the offeror is intoxicated or joking and he offers to sell his business. The offeree cannot accept the offeror's suggestion and scoop up the business from the offeror by these words alone.

Another time when an offer is not made is when the offeror makes an invitation to submit an offer. For example, an advertisement in the paper to purchase an item is not an offer, but rather an invitation to the public to make an offer. To qualify as an offer, there must be definite terms. For example, the subject matter, price, quantity, persons intended as the offeree, and terms should be discussed.

Although, sometimes nonessential terms can be left out and trade usage will apply common terms and make the offer valid.

Offer Still Open? Once an offer is made it remains open until accepted or terminated by revocation of the offeror or rejection by the offeree. For example, say I made an offer to sell you this book for one dollar, but then thought about how much work it was and decided that one dollar was not sufficient to meet my needs. If I contact you before you accept my price of one dollar and tell you that the offer is off, you can no longer accept my offer and purchase the book for one dollar. This is because I have revoked my offer.

On the other hand, say that I kept the price at one dollar, but you decided you wanted to buy thousands of copies because you want to use the book in a teaching setting. Thus, you said that you would purchase at least one thousand copies at fifty cents each. This is a counteroffer which, in essence, cuts off my offer. Instead, your counteroffer becomes the offer and now I become the offeree and have the power of acceptance. This offer/counteroffer area of the law is quite complicated and much litigation results because of it, so do not be alarmed if this sounds confusing, because it is.

Offer Accepted? As mentioned, the offer stays open until acceptance, rejection, or revocation. The only one that has the power to accept the offer is the one to whom the offer is made. For example, if I made an offer to sell you a BMW for ten thousand dollars, you are the only one who can accept that offer.

Consideration. In addition to offer and acceptance, there must be consideration in order to create a legally binding contract. Consideration is the bargain for exchange, i.e., it is the legal duty undertaken by each party that he or she is not obligated to do. For example, in the above example where I offer to sell you a car, my consideration is giving up the car and yours is giving up the money. Now, the above example regarding the sale of this book for one dollar may not be sufficient if you were my brother and it was really a disguised gift. This is because the consideration given must be valuable, and nominal consideration may not be sufficient to form a contract.

Offeree Have Capacity? In addition to the above, the offeree must have capacity to accept the offer. Those who do not have capacity include minors (in some instances) and those who are intoxicated.

Against Public Policy? A contract will not be formed if it is against public policy. For example, if the contract is heavily weighted in favor of the stronger party in its terms and in its negotiation, the contract may be deemed unconscionable and void as against public policy.

No Fraud, Certain Mistakes. If a party is induced into making a contract because of fraud or certain mistakes, courts may find no contract and therefore release the defrauded or mistaken party from the contract.

Once Formed, What Are Your Obligations?

Absolute Duty. Once a contract is created, each party has the absolute duty to perform his or her obligations under the contract, unless his or her duty does not ripen until certain conditions are met or unless his or her duty is discharged.

Conditions? Sometimes parties to a contract perform at the same time. Other times one party has to perform his or her duty before the other party is obligated. For example, if I sell you a BMW, our duties ripen at the same time as I hand over the keys and car and you hand over the money. However, what if I had a loan on the car? Then, you would probably request that I pay off the loan before the sale or as part of the sale. Thus, your duty to purchase would not rise until the loan is paid off. This is known as a condition, and all conditions must either be satisfied or excused before your duty ripens.

Duty Discharged? Sometimes supervening events occur that allow a party's duty to be discharged. For example, if an earthquake hits and your business is among the rubble, then it is possible that your duty will be excused and you will be released from the contract. However, a duty is only discharged if the supervening event arises after formation of the contract and only if it was unforeseeable.

Breach? If the other party breaches, you may or may not be released from performing. If the breach was minor, you may have to perform. However, you should be able to gain something from the breach. For example, say you have contracted to build your own house and you and the contractor agreed on copper plumbing. If the contractor completes the house to your specifications with one minor change—not using copper plumbing—you would probably have to complete the purchase. However, you will also probably receive a reduction in how much you had to pay. In another situation, if the other party committed a material breach, you may have to allow him or her time to cure before the breach ripens into a total breach whereby you can be released from the contract. Such a situation might be if you ordered one hundred thousand cases of tissue paper, and the other party sent you one hundred cases of paper towels.

What are your remedies for failure to perform? If you are wronged in a contract, you may have a plethora of remedies available to you. You may be able to rescind the contract, obtain money damages, get an injunction to force a party to stop doing something, or obtain an order for specific performance to force a party to continue doing something. Additionally, you may be able to rescind the contract and then request the value of the benefit conferred, which is known as restitution.

The following mini-test will provide you with additional insight into contract issues:

Mini-Test Regarding Contracts

1. An accountant promises to prepare an attorney's tax returns in exchange for the attorney's promise to incorporate the accountant's sole proprietorship. No cash is part of the transaction. Has a contract been formed?

2. A business owner promises not to purchase copy paper from other vendors in return for a particular vendor's promise to supply the business owner with all his requirements for copy paper. Has a contract been formed?

3. John Q. Public goes to a BMW dealership and test drives a new convertible. He likes the car and hands the salesman a check for $35,000 and tells him to get the car ready and he'll be back in a few hours to pick it up. The car is ready when Mr. Public returns, but he tells the salesman that he changed his mind and the deal is off and he demands his money back. Can he get it?

4. You ask a painter to paint your office building for flat fee of $5,000. The next day you leave town on a business trip, and while you're away, you decide to put off the painting job. When you return, the job's finished. Do you have to pay for it even though the painter

never communicated whether he'd do the job or not, but rather just went ahead and painted?

5. You are the owner of a stereo store. A minor comes in and purchases a $2,500 car stereo on credit. You install it in his car and he makes one payment and refuses to make more. Can you enforce the contract?

Answers to Mini-Test Regarding Contracts

1. A contract is formed in a variety of ways. One of those ways is when one party promises to do something for another party's promise to do something. In our example, a contract is formed because the accountant promises to provide accounting services in exchange for the attorney's promise to provide legal services.

2. One way a contract can be formed is when one party promises not to do something in exchange for another party's promise to do something. In our example, a contract is formed because the business owner promises not to purchase from other vendors so long as the supplier supplies the owner with all the owner's requirements for copy paper.

3. Some contracts must be in writing to be enforceable. One type is a contract that covers the sale of goods worth five hundred dollars or more. In our example the contract is unenforceable because the sale is for a car worth $35,000 and no written contract was signed. Therefore, the salesman must give the purchaser his money back. Other contracts that must be in writing include: 1) a contract that covers real property and any buildings on real property; 2) a contract that cannot, by its terms, be performed within one year of its making; and 3) a contract to guarantee the debt of another, if the guarantor's obligation is collateral. (Some exceptions apply to all of the above listed situations, but it is nevertheless a good idea to get all of your contracts in writing.)

4. Contracts can be bilateral or unilateral. Bilateral contracts occur where one party promises to do or not to do something for the other party's promise to do or not to do something. On the other hand, unilateral contracts occur where one party promises to do something in exchange for the other party's performance of an act. In some states, the second party does not have to communicate his acceptance. Instead, he accepts the offer by completing the full act.

In our example, a contract is created upon completion of the painting because the business owner promises to pay $5,000 in exchange for having his building painted. He does not call the painter to revoke his offer, and in the meantime, the painter completes the act, and therefore is entitled to payment. If the situation was that the painter had only finished half of the building when the owner returned, modern law would give the painter the opportunity to complete his performance, and at completion, he would be entitled to full payment.

5. There are certain defenses to making a contract. One is where a person does not have the capacity to enter into a contract. A minor fits in this category, and it doesn't matter if he may have looked older or represented himself to be older. A business owner cannot force him to pay. In our example, the minor could void the contract because he lacked capacity to enter into the contract and therefore could not be held liable to complete his performance. However, the business owner would have a remedy under another area of law known as unjust enrichment. Additionally, there's an exception to this rule for minors which occurs if a minor enters into a contract for necessities, he's liable for the reasonable value of the necessities. Thus, if a seventeen year old rents an apartment, he's liable for reasonable value of lease term.

How to Negotiate a Contract

Negotiating can be fun if you understand five basic premises: first, do not take anything personally; second, understand that timing is everything; third, prepare, prepare, and prepare; fourth, know where the power lies; and fifth, care, but not that much.

Do Not Take Anything Personally

Business issues are separate issues from the people. Keep reminding yourself of the issues and what goals you are trying to accomplish. Never lose sight of why you are in negotiations. Attacking someone personally will get you nowhere. Do not get angry and do not be afraid to ask questions. Do not let the other side bully you. Keep your focus on the issues and ignore bullying tactics until they lose their sting. It will happen, just be patient.

If the situation gets too bad, make an excuse to leave or hang up the telephone—do anything but show the other person is getting to you. Analyze why the other side employs such tactics. What pressures does he or she face? What does he or she want? Understand that the other side is no different than you, in that each of you 1) may be fearful or not particularly like the negotiation process, and 2) has needs which are not necessarily opposite. Find out the other side's needs and help them meet their needs, while at the same time making sure that you get what you want—just because you are helping another to meet their needs does not mean that less of your needs will be met.

Timing Is Everything

Chances are that as a child, you knew when to ask for your allowance, or when to drive the family car, or when to beg for forgiveness to get your privileges back. Well, timing is everything in any negotiation and you should keep in mind that the same news can have a very different effect when presented at different times. If possible, negotiate when the other side is happy and when you are in a good mood. Never negotiate when you are tired. Break bad news at the proper time, and if possible, soften the blow with a preface of good news.

Also, most negotiations happen as close to the deadline as possible, so be patient and wait for the 11th hour. As you approach a deadline, understand that a shift of power may occur and you may find yourself in a better (or worse) bargaining position. So, get to know the other side's deadline as soon as possible and figure out if the deadline is real—you may find out that it is more flexible than what you first thought.

Prepare, Prepare, and Prepare

Prenegotiations are as important as the formal negotiating event itself. Use the time prior to formal negotiations to ask questions and obtain as much information as possible because such information translates into power. Once you have enough information, access your leverage and determine your course of action. If others perceive you as having more knowledge than they have, they will respect you.

Also, remember that negotiation is a two-way street and you will need to provide information to the other side. Do not be afraid to provide the information as it will probably help you more than it will hurt you (because information provided at the formal event for the first time is not usually received well—people need time to digest the information).

Know Where the Power Lies

Some people will not negotiate a contract because of the power of print. Do not be afraid to challenge the written word when it's to your advantage to do so, and vice versa, use written language when it's advantageous to do so. Also, understand that power lies in spending time. For example, if you walk onto a used car lot and up to a salesman and immediately ask him to cut the sticker price of a $40,000 BMW to $35,000, you will probably get a quick "no," whereas, if you spend some time with the salesman and come back on a couple of occasions, you may walk out with the deal that you wanted. Lastly, power lies in knowledge—so know what you are talking about or act like you know what you are talking about.

Care, But Not That Much

One of the cardinal rules in negotiation is not to negotiate for yourself. This may be because people tend to care too much when they negotiate for themselves. Do not snap at the bait no matter how tempting it may be. If the other side knows that you want but do not need the deal, you will be in a better bargaining position. Keep an even keel and keep negotiating.

Caveat Emptor Isn't Just for Buyers Anymore

Last year, millions of people signed contracts. This year, many of those signatories will lose thousands of dollars litigating over them. Why? Because some will not read the recitals and boilerplate, others will scan only the first few paragraphs of the contract, and still others will read the entire contract but will not understand the terms that they read. Many of these people will sign on the dotted line and turn their signed deals into sour deals. Don't let this happen to you. Remember the term caveat emptor? Well, the buyer isn't the only one these days who should be aware of what he or she is signing. Whether you are a company executive or employee, a buyer or seller, a landlord or tenant, or a contractor or subcontractor, you should be aware of what you are signing before you put yourself (and possibly others) at risk. Here are some tips to take with you:

Recitals

The recitals are located at the beginning of the contract and state the names of the parties and what each party is going to provide under the terms of the contract. Sometimes they begin with the word "whereas." Pay attention to recitals, because in some states, they are deemed to be admissions of the parties, that without contrary evidence, are presumed to be true. For example, if the recitals state that you will act as the agent of a third party and not as a principal for yourself, then you had better act in the capacity as an agent, or you may wind up in litigation.

Remedies

The general rule in many states, remedies are cumulative unless explicitly stated otherwise. Therefore, any or all remedies may be granted under the same contract. So, if you want to limit remedies, make sure the contract indicates such limits. Also, there are times when courts will limit remedies. For example, when the requirements of a contract limit remedies by implication, some courts may limit them accordingly. So, if a subcontractor signs a contract stating that he will not delay or cease work if a dispute erupts between him and the general contractor, then the subcontractor may unknowingly have limited his remedies to bringing a breach of contract action, which may not be his best remedy.

Unconscionable Contracts

A contract that is extremely unfair to one party in the negotiation process and in the terms of the contract is called an unconscionable contract. In many states, courts generally refuse to enforce unconscionable contracts, or they enforce them without the unconscionable clauses. However, as applied to remedies, some courts do not seem so willing to throw out unconscionable clauses. For example, in a case where a party "waived all rights to recover damages," the court found that neither the contract nor the clause was commercially unreasonable, so the party lost all rights to recover damages. So, make sure that you do not waive all your rights to recourse, because you might get what you bargained for.

Liquidated Damages

Liquidated damages clauses frequently grant the parties the right to seek an injunction for breach of contract and to receive money damages that are spelled out in the contract. In most states, liquidated damages must be reasonable under the circumstances at the time the contract is formed or the courts will not allow them. Therefore, if you enter into a contract worth hundreds, don't use a liquidating damages clause that escalates into thousands of dollars or you might end up without any liquidated money damages at all. Instead, make sure that the amount of liquidated damages are reasonable so the courts will not deem them a penalty and deny them.

Also, for liquidated damages to be considered reasonable in some states, the parties must have calculated or estimated actual damages. Moreover, liquidated damage clauses are not allowed in certain contracts (e.g. those involving personal, family, or household rentals, or retail purposes). Furthermore, contrary to popular belief, liquidating damages clauses will not limit other remedies.

Arbitration

For some time now, parties have been adding arbitration clauses to their contracts stating that they would settle any controversy or claim by arbitration instead of litigation. This is perhaps because some state statutes and case law seem to favor arbitration. However, whether or not to include an arbitration clause should be a personal decision. Proponents use arbitration clauses because they believe the process is less expensive and faster than bringing their case to a court of law.

Those against arbitration believe that the process takes just as long as litigation, that some arbitrators are not qualified, and that most of the time, the case is just split and all parties end up paying, even when it is clear that one party is not at fault. Some arbitration clauses are binding and others are not. However, once arbitration is in place, courts generally will not interfere with the process. Once a final decision has been made by the arbitrator, courts usually limit their review to the validity of the arbitration award and whether or not the arbitrator acted with misconduct or fraud.

Attorney Fees

Parties to a contract can get their attorney's fees paid under two conditions: 1) if it is statutory, and 2) if the contract provides for such fees. However, attorney's fees language in some contracts is so vague, sometimes it does not cover fees that the parties intended, and other times it covers more than what the parties intended. For example, many contracts use language similar to the following: "Should it be necessary to institute a cause of action to enforce the terms of this agreement, the parties agree that the prevailing party shall be entitled to reasonable attorney's fees." Used alone, this sentence is too vague. It does not state what actions are covered or what claims can be filed, nor does it limit the amount of damages that a party can receive. Furthermore, it lacks anti-merger language to cover post-judgment collection and enforcement actions, and language regarding fees on appeal (which would not be granted if not stated).

Rather than use such a vague statement, perhaps it would be better to tailor your attorney's fees clauses to fit the needs of each contract. A word of caution for those who cut and paste agreements together: you could end up losing attorney's fees altogether. Take the above sample sentence, and note the words "a cause of action." Now, if this sentence is used in a contract that contains an arbitration clause requiring the parties to arbitrate their differences, then the prevailing party may not end up getting his or her fees paid, because "cause of action" usually refers to litigation and not arbitration. On the positive side, if an attorney's fees clause is one-sided, courts will deem the rights to be reciprocal.

Costs

Costs are another area where contracts are often too vague. For example, the statement that "the prevailing party shall recover all costs" is too vague for most situations. However, many contracts will use such language and the result has sometimes been costly. In one case, a court denied costs of expert witnesses (usually the most expensive court costs) because it was not specifically provided for in the contract.

Entire Agreement

Too many people have signed a contract believing that the written word includes the verbal representations made by the other party, but found out too late that the two were quite different. If the contract had a "zipper clause" in it, the party may lose the benefit of the oral representations. Why? Because a zipper clause states that the agreement reflects the final expression of the parties' agreement and its terms supersede all previous verbal and written agreements. Therefore, if a party verbally says one thing, but the written contract says another, the written contract will prevail if it contains a zipper clause (if no exceptions apply). So, if the other party does not want to put his or her representations in writing, watch out—you probably will not get what you bargained for.

Governing Law

With parties transacting business not only across state lines, but now overseas, parties need to be aware of what laws govern their contracts. Usually, there is a clause in the contract stating the parties agree that all questions respecting the contract, or the rights, obligations, and liabilities of the parties to the contract, are determined in accordance with applicable laws of a certain state or nation. Make sure that you know which state or nation's laws apply because it could make a difference in how you are protected.

Jurisdictional Consent

It used to be that forum selection clauses were deemed by the courts to be invalid. Forum selection clauses state that the parties consent to jurisdiction in a certain state or nation. Now, most federal and some state courts generally enforce such clauses where the parties freely negotiate them and where the jurisdiction is not unreasonable and unjust. So, if you are located in California, but signed a contract in New York, and the contract states that any action involving the contract will be brought in New York, you had better be prepared to travel to New York, because you consented to its jurisdiction. This is especially so in California, where courts have said that mere inconvenience is not an adequate reason to withhold enforcement of a forum selection clause. So, be careful where you consent to jurisdiction.

Modification

It is a good idea to include a clause to the effect that a contract can only be amended or modified if the amendment or modification is expressed in a writing signed by all the parties. If you include such a clause, then make sure you follow its mandate, because if you orally change the terms of a contract, it is possible that neither you nor the other party will have to abide by the changes.

Non-Waiver

If you have been a party to numerous contracts, chances are that the situation has come up whereby 1) you have allowed the other party to forego a payment, 2) you have accepted a late payment, or 3) you have been granted an extension or forgiveness of a payment from the other party.

So that being a nice person does not cost you your rights, make sure to include a clause in your contracts to the effect that if you fail to insist upon prompt and punctual performance of any term or condition, or if you fail to exercise any right or remedy under the terms of the contract, that such failure will not constitute a waiver of that or any other term, condition, right, or remedy on that or any subsequent occasion. Providing such a clause will assist you in not waiving your rights to future payments or to payments being made on time.

Severability

Sometimes a court will declare a provision of a contract to be unenforceable or invalid for various reasons. Such a declaration may have an effect on making the whole contract null and void. To assist in preventing this from happening, you can draft a clause to the effect that if any provision is held by a court to be unenforceable or invalid for any reason, that the remaining provisions of the agreement will be unaffected by such holding. Therefore, if one provision is deemed unenforceable, at least the contract stands and the parties will have to abide by the other terms in the contract.

These are just a few tips to be aware of before you enter into your next negotiating deal. There are many others, the most of which is not to be afraid to ask questions if you do not understand the language in some of the clauses.

Getting Out of Contracts

Now that you understand a little more about contract clauses, you are better equipped to enter into your next contract. However, there may still be times when you feel that you have been wronged. If that is the case, you have the following options:

- Check consumer protection laws and consumer agencies that handle contractual problems.
- Bring the contract to the attorney general's office where fraud is involved.
- Bring the contract to an attorney who specializes in contract law to get his or her evaluation.

Intellectual Property

Another area where business owners need to protect their backsides is the intellectual property area, which includes copyrights, trademarks, trade names, and patents. Copyrights protect the originality of authorship, like writings from an author; trademarks protect a source of origin of goods and services, like the golden arches shows a hungry person where to get a McDonald's® hamburger; trade names identify a person, business, or occupation, like General Motors® identifies the automaker who manufactures Chevrolets®; and patents protect novel inventions or discoveries, like the Macintosh® Powerbook computers.

Copyrights

This section explains the basics about copyrights. It provides answers to copyright registration and infringement of copyrights. But first, let's take a test to determine if the following situations warrant copyright protection.

Mini-Test Regarding Copyright Issues

1. You've written a book on the civil war. You haven't discussed anything new that others before you haven't written about and some of the incidents between the two writings sound similar. However, your writing is of your own making. Is your book copyrightable?

2. You're a motivational speaker who has presented the same oral speech to various businesses hundreds of times around the country. Is the speech copyrightable?

3. You own a bakery and sell the world's best chocolate chip and peanut butter cookies. You write down the recipes and want to copyright them. Are they copyrightable?

4. You have an idea for a television show and you want to get it protected before you disclose it to the networks. Can you obtain copyright protection on your idea?

5. You're in the business of making jewelry. You design many animal pins. Can you obtain copyright protection for the pins?

Answers to Mini-Test Regarding Copyright Issues

1. One factor in obtaining copyright protection is that a work must be original. In our example, the work is similar to others, but is the original thoughts of the author and therefore copyrightable if it fits one of the categories of works that are copyrightable. Those categories comprise the following: sound recordings, pantomimes, choreographic works, pictorial, graphic and sculptural works, motion pictures, audiovisual works, musical works, dramatic works, architectural works, and literary works. Since the book in this example is a literary work, it would qualify for copyright protection.

2. To be copyrightable, a work must not only be original, but it must also be fixed in any tangible form. Therefore, until the speech in our example is written down or recorded, it's not copyrightable.

3. Some works cannot be protected by copyright; included in this category are lists of ingredients, contents, or as a general rule, forms. Since the recipes in this example are a list of ingredients, they are not copyrightable. However, one might be able to obtain copyright protection if he or she compiles the recipes in a recipe book, and creates enough originality in the book. Other works which cannot be protected by copyright include: 1) titles of works, names of products or services, even if they are novel or distinctive; 2) names of businesses, organizations, or groups; 3) catch words, slogans, short phrases, and familiar symbols for familiar designs; and 4) information that is in the public domain (common property and property that

contains no original authorship) such as standard charts, measuring devices, and tables or lists taken from government public sources.

4. In our example, we're trying to copyright an idea. Some works cannot be protected by copyright and ideas are one of them. However, expressions of ideas are copyrightable, so if in our example, we were trying to copyright the program format, it would probably be protectable. If this idea/expression dichotomy confuses you, don't feel bad because it's one of the most litigated areas of the law of copyright and experts are confused over it, so you're not alone. Other areas where you cannot obtain copyright protection include systems, processes, procedures, concepts, or methods. The reason that the copyright laws will not protect these areas is because they do not have the requisite originality of expression to distinguish them from the ideas they represent.

5. Jewelry is a work of visual art. Other examples of visual art include sculpture, toys, artwork on plates, and fabric or textile attached to or part of a three-dimensional object such as furniture. Copyright laws extend to such works, and therefore, in our example the jewelry would be copyrightable.

Protecting Your Copyrights

Now that you understand more about copyrights in general, let's discuss how to protect your copyrights, because when people talk about "copyrighting a work" they either mean putting a notice on the work or they mean registering the copyright. Surprisingly, today neither is needed to create copyright protection. Rather, protection exists as soon as the original work is put into tangible form. So, why use the notice symbol and register the copyright?

Notice of Copyright

The copyright notice includes three parts: 1) the symbol ©, or "copyright" or "copr"; 2) year of creation; and 3) name of owner. It can be placed anywhere where it provides reasonable notice that the copyright is being claimed. For example, on a book, it's usually on the inside cover or on one of the first few pages, and on a computer program, it's usually on the first screen or in the source code or object code. On television or radio commercials, it need not appear on the screen or be broadcast over the air waves. Instead, the notice is placed on the cassette or script.

For works created before March 31, 1989, notice is a prerequisite to obtaining copyright protection. Therefore, for those works, you must use the notice or the copyright will fall into what is known as the "public domain," which means that the work cannot be protected by copyright and anyone can copy it. However, for works created after March 31, 1989, notice is not required, but the owner should use it for three very good reasons:

1) Without it, the owner would have to prove his or her damages in a copyright infringement lawsuit, whereas with it, the owner would be allowed to obtain statutory damages and therefore proof of damages is not necessary.

2) Without it, the owner would not be able to get his attorney's fees and court costs paid if he prevails in a copyright infringement lawsuit, where with it his attorney's fees and court costs would be paid if he wins.

3) An infringer cannot claim he or she innocently infringed upon your work.

Copyright Registration

Why register if it's not necessary to preserve a copyright? The answer is threefold:

1) In the United States, no lawsuit can be brought for copyright infringement until a work is registered. This means if you see someone else has copied your work, you cannot sue them until you register the work.

2) Certain remedies in a court of law would not be available to you. These remedies include your attorney's fees being paid and statutory damages being awarded to you if you prevailed in an infringement suit.

3) Registration provides prima facie evidence that the facts in the registration documents are true, which shifts the burden of proof concerning those facts from the copyright owner to the defendant in a lawsuit.

Who can register? The author who created the work, the owner of exclusive rights if the work has been transferred, or the authorized agent of the copyright owner.

What's needed to register? The correct form properly filled out according to the instructions that are included with the form, which is signed by one of the three persons listed as claimants. The form is deposited with one or two copies of the work (or a deposit showing the work, in the case of three-dimensional or extra-large works) and the filing fee.

Where do you register? All of the above items must be sent to the Register of Copyrights, at the Copyright Office, located in the Library of Congress, Washington, DC 20559.

When is registration effective? On the date the copyright office receives all of the required materials in acceptable form.

When does a copyright expire? For works created on or after January 1, 1978, life of the claimant plus 50 years. When two or more authors create a joint work, the life of the last surviving author plus 50 years. If the copyright was prepared within the scope of employment, 75 years from the date of first publication or 100 years from the date of creation, whichever comes first. For works created prior to January 1, 1978, basically 75 years from first publication (if renewed at 28 years after first published).

Copyright Infringement

Copyright protects the following rights: to copy the works, to prepare derivative works, to distribute the works, to publicly perform the works, and to put the works on public display. There are exceptions to these rights. However, they are too complicated to explain here. Generally, suffice it to say that anyone who violates rights of the copyright owner is liable for copyright infringement in a lawsuit which is brought in a federal court.

Ownership and Copying

In an infringement action, the owner of copyrighted material (plaintiff) must establish ownership and copying by the infringer (defendant) of plaintiff's copyrighted work to establish copyright infringement. Since it is rare that actual evidence of copying exists, the courts show proof of copying by a two-part test: access and substantial similarity.

First, the copyright owner must prove that the infringer had access to the copyrighted work. Then, the owner must show that the two works are so similar that the ordinary person would conclude the defendant unlawfully appropriated plaintiff's protectable expression by taking material of substance and value. The courts balance access with substantial similarity, so if the copyright owner has greater evidence of access, he or she needs less proof of substantial similarity, and vice versa.

Remedies

A copyright owner who prevails in a copyright infringement action has two remedies available to him or her: injunction and damages. By obtaining an injunction, the owner is able to prevent the infringement from continuing, and this is usually more important to the owner than obtaining monetary damages, because of obvious reasons. Damages may be awarded in two alternative ways. The first is actual damages and profits, which means the owner is entitled to recover his or her actual damages and any profits of the infringer that are attributable to the infringement. (Profits are recoverable only if and to the extent that such profits are not included in actual damages.) In the alternative, and provided that the proper procedures were followed, the owner may obtain statutory damages. These damages are currently measured at $500 to $20,000 for each work infringed upon, or if plaintiff proves willful infringement, he or she may have the amount increased to $100,000.

Trademarks

A trademark is anything which identifies and distinguishes the goods and services of one's business. If the mark is used to identify a service, the mark is called a service mark. In general, trademarks appear on the product or on the packaging and service marks appear in advertising, such as on business cards, stationery, letterhead, signs. This section explains the basics about trademarks and service marks, and it provides answers to questions regarding trademark registration and infringement of such marks. But first, let's take a test to determine whether you think a mark is trademarkable.

Mini-Test Regarding Trademarks

1. You're a tobacco manufacturer and you wrap cigars in wrappers from the United States, and put the word "Havana" on the cigar boxes. Can you use "Havana" as your trademark?

2. You're the only baker in your county and you want to trademark the word "bread." Can you trademark it?

3. You're in the computer software business, and you want to provide a slogan as your trademark. Can you do that?

4. You have an artist design a logo for your business, and you want to use it as your trademark. Can you do so?

5. You arbitrarily throw a lot of letters together to make up a word. Is your arbitrary word trademarkable?

Answers to Mini-Test Regarding Trademarks

1. Certain marks cannot be protected by trademark. Included in this category are marks which are primarily geographically descriptive of the goods or services. In our example, the mark could not be used as your trademark since the wrappers were not from Cuba, and to use such a mark would be geographically deceptive. Other marks which cannot be protected by trademark include the following: 1) any mark that is immoral, deceptive, or scandalous; 2) any mark that falsely suggests that a person or business is connected to the mark when this is not the case; and 3) any mark which does not identify the source of the goods or service.

2. The generic name of a product is not trademarkable because a competitor would be excluded from using a word that he or she needs to communicate the product that he or she offers. In our example, we wouldn't be able to trademark the word "bread" because it is the common name for the product and it cannot be tied only to one source. It's interesting to note that trademarks can lose their

trademark status if they become generic. Examples of lost trademarks include "thermos," "aspirin," and "cellophane." The Xerox Corporation seems to be fighting this situation today. It appears that they are instructing their employees, agents, customers, and the public in general advertising, to use the mark as a proper adjective in conjunction with the product or service. For example, they might say, "Please make ten Xerox copies of this document," and not just say, "Please Xerox ten of these documents."

3. Many types of marks can be trademarked, and slogans are included in this category. In our example, you could develop a slogan to be used in advertising and also use it as a source in identifying your mark. AT&T and American Express have done such a thing with their slogans of "The Right Choice" and "Don't leave home without it."

4. Another type of mark which can used as a trademark includes a symbol, which may comprise of letters or numbers or a combination of the two. Examples of symbols used as registered trademarks include "GE" used by General Electric, "3M" used by the 3M Corporation, and "7-Eleven" used by The Southland Corporation. Additionally, a symbol may include label designs like the triangle on Guess Jeans or characters like Mickey Mouse. A symbol can also include a company logo, and therefore, in our example, it would be possible to trademark the logo.

5. Words are probably the most popular form of trademarks and the more arbitrary and fanciful a word, the stronger the trademark will be. Thus, in our example, the arbitrary word would gain the strongest protection under trademark laws. This is because such marks are generally created just for trademark purposes. An example of an arbitrary word created for trademark purposes is "Exxon." Another category of marks are those which are suggestive, which, while not really descriptive of the product's qualities, nevertheless suggest some benefit or property of the product. They are the next strongest category of marks. An example would be to use "soft" for tissue paper. Descriptive words are another category of marks. They can be protected by trademark registration only after the owner shows that it is the source of the mark. Finally, words not protected by trademark law are those which we have already discussed in question two: words which are generic or have become the generic word for the product itself.

Trademark Registration

Is Registration Required for Trademark Protection?

No. However, you should register your mark for the following reasons: 1) without registration, you will leave yourself open to losing the right to use the mark; 2) failing to register may be a basis for the Trademark Office's refusal to register the mark later on; 3) without registration, another person or entity may acquire superior rights over you; and 4) you don't have the right to sue in federal court for trademark infringement without registration.

Federal vs. State Registration

In most instances, you will be selling your goods and services across state lines, and thus you'll need to seek federal registration. For the few of you who will restrict your sales and services to intrastate activity, you can seek state registration.

What Is the Federal Registration Process?

To be eligible for registration at the federal registry, you must sell your goods or services across state lines. The application that you will use will depend on your current situation. If you are using the mark on goods or in selling your services, you will prepare an In-Use Application. To be eligible to use the In-Use Application, you will have to show that you are using the mark in the ordinary course of trade and not merely reserving a right in the mark.

If you have not yet begun to use the mark, but have merely selected it to use in the future, you must fill out an Intent-To-Use Application and state that you have a bona fide intent to use the mark on the goods or in advertising services. Once you file the Intent-to-Use Application, you must file a follow-up statement within six months. If you started to use the mark, the statement will be a "Statement-Of-Use." If you haven't used the mark, you will file for an extension, but you must show proper bona fide efforts in order to have the extension granted. You may be granted a total of six extensions before your Intent-To-Use Application will expire.

On grant of a registration, the original filing of the Intent-To-Use Application will be the date that the Trademark Office uses to show constructive priority of the mark. To obtain the proper application form from the United States Patent and Trademark Office, contact the U.S. Department of Commerce, Patent and Trademark Office, Washington, DC 20231.

Your application starts its journey through the Trademark Office at the mail room, where a clerk reviews the application, specimens, drawings, and filing fee to see if each meets the filing requirements, and if so, the clerk forwards the application package to one of several law offices which are located in the Trademark Office. The mail clerk also sends you a filing receipt with a filing date and serial number for your mark. Once you have this receipt and number, you can call the Trademark Office status line to obtain information on where your application is at any given time. At the law office, an examining attorney is assigned to the mark to determine its eligibility.

This review takes about three to six months, and if the mark is approved, it is published in the Official Gazette (which is the principal registration for all trademarks) for 30 days. If no person challenges the mark within that time period, a trademark registration certificate is issued and the trademark is granted. If the examining attorney rejects the mark, he or she will send an action letter to the applicant stating the reasons for the rejection and the applicant will have six months to respond to the attorney's rejection. Upon receiving the applicant's written response to the action letter, the trademark examining attorney will either reverse the rejection or remain strong in his or her position and deny registration. If the latter occurs, the applicant would have to appeal the attorney's decision to the Trademark Trial and Appeals Board.

When Does a Federal Trademark Expire?

Trademarks or service marks which were filed after November 19, 1989, are good for a term of ten years with ten year renewal terms. However, in order to take advantage of the renewal terms, the trademark owner must, between the fifth and sixth year after the date of registration, file an affidavit stating that the mark is currently being used. If the trademark owner fails to prepare and file the affidavit, the registration will be canceled and the owner will lose the mark. The trademark owner must be careful not to let his or her mark be can-celed, because trademark "pirates" watch for this to occur and scoop up the trademark as soon as it is expired and they'll be more than happy to sell it back to the owner for a premium.

What Is the State Registration Process?

Registration of state trademarks is handled by one of two state offices: either 1) the Trademark Office, or 2) the Secretary of State. You need to check with your state to determine which is the correct agency to contact. The registration process is basically the same as for federal trademarks. However, most states will only allow a mark to be registered if it is in use.

How Long Is a State Trademark Effective?

Like the federal registration process, most states offer protection for a term of ten years, with ten year renewal periods, wherein the owner has a duty to contact the state within the fifth to sixth year to show that he or she is still using the mark. If you are interested in obtaining a state trademark, you should check with the appropriate state agency to obtain further details.

When Is a Trademark or Service Mark Lost?

When the owner stops using the mark or does not stop others from using it.

What Is the Trademark Symbol?

The correct trademark symbol after registration of the mark at either the federal or state level is ®, or "Registered in the U.S. Patent & Trademark Office" or "Reg. U.S. Pat. & TM Off." If the mark is in registration process or if it is not registered, the trademark owner may only use the symbol TM for trademarks or SM for service marks to indicate a claim of ownership. Under no circumstances should the trademark owner use the ®, or "Registered in the U.S. Patent & Trademark Office" or "Reg. U.S. Pat. & TM Off." prior to completing the registration process. If one of these symbols are used prior to registration, the owner may be denied a subsequent registration.

Trademark Infringement

The test for trademark infringement is known as "likelihood of confusion." It means if the general public is likely to think that your product or service comes from another company that is unrelated to you, that your product or service infringes on the other company's. Some of the factors that are used to determine likelihood of confusion are as follows:

1) The strength of the mark.
2) The similarity of the marks as displayed on the goods, or in connection with the services.
3) The likelihood that consumers would expect the new product to come from the old owner.
4) The presence of actual confusion.
5) The channels of trade.
6) The degree of sophistication of consumers.
7) The similarity of the marks or similarity in advertising the marks.
8) The second user's good faith in adopting its mark.

How Do You Avoid Infringement When Referring to Marks?

When you refer to one's trademark or service mark, make it clear that the mark is registered to the respective holder. To do this, place the symbol "®" after every mark, then place an asterisk after the symbol, and at the bottom of the same page, explain that the mark is a registered trademark or service mark of the respective holder. If you follow this procedure for every mark that you refer to, and if you make it clear that you're not claiming ownership of the mark, but rather only using or referring to it, you should be fine. For example, one might indicate a trademark as follows: "Accel-a-Writer®*," then, at the bottom of the page, state, "*Accel-a-Writer® is a trademark of XANTE Corporation."

Patents

To promote the progress of science, the U.S. Constitution grants inventors an exclusive right to exclude everyone else from using, making, or selling their invention. This right is known as having a "patent" and the societal benefit is that after the patent expires, it is free for public use. This section explains the basics about patents and provides answers to the most frequently asked questions.

What Can Be Protected by a Patent?

A product, process, method, machine, manufacture, composition, and any useful improvement thereof; and an ornamental design for an article of manufacture.

What Is Not Patentable?

Laws of nature scientific principles, mathematical formulas, methods of doing business, and an improvement in a device that only takes mechanical skills to develop.

How Do You Obtain a Patent?

If you are the inventor, you can obtain a patent application from the U.S. Patent and Trademark Office, located at The U.S. Department of Commerce, Patent and Trademark Office, Washington, DC 20231. If you're an individual or small business, ask for a declaration of patent application, a verified statement claiming small entity status, and an application transmittal letter. These documents are used together for registration of federal patents.

Prepare your application according to the instructions that accompany the application and file the application as well as the correct filing fee with the above agency. (Make sure that you contact them for the correct filing fee as it varies and depends on numerous factors.) If you are not the inventor, you may not obtain a patent. The inventor may subsequently sell his interest in the patent to you, but the application must still be filed in the inventor's name.

When Is the Inventor Prevented from Getting a Patent?

A patent may not be obtained if the invention was in public use or for sale in the United States for more than one year prior to filing the patent application.

How Long Is a Patent Good?

A patent is generally granted for a term of 17 years (although this is changing to 20 years as a result of GATT). However, a design patent may be good for 14 years. Once the patent expires, the owner loses the exclusive rights to the invention and it becomes available for public use.

What Does "Patent Pending" Mean?

It is an indication that the patent application is on file with the patent office. It may be a deterrent to others to apply for a patent on the same patent claims, but it does not give the inventor protection under patent laws.

Trade Name Protection

A trade name is something that is used to identify a person, business, occupation, or vocation. It can be a name, word, symbol, device, or a combination of the same. A trade name differs from a trademark because it identifies goods and services, in addition to the trademark owner's business, occupation, or vocation, and a trademark only identifies goods and services.

An example of using a trade name in conjunction with a trademark is the trademark Chevrolet® and the trade name General Motors®. There is no federal registration of a trade name, but some states protect trade names by providing for filing of Fictitious Business Name Statements. If you are interested in registering a trade name, you should check with the appropriate state agency to determine if your state registers such names.

Licensing

Once you have obtained protection under patent, trademark, or copyright laws, you have the exclusive right to sell your intellectual property right to another person or business. You can do this by selling it outright or by licensing the right to use the property. If you choose to license the property, the license can be sold to one person or entity, or to more than one.

If you grant a license, there are several questions to consider. For example, you need to decide what specific property you want to license. You need to make sure steps have been taken to protect that property. For example, has the property been registered at the U.S. Copyright or Patent and Trademarks registry? What about international registration? Another question to ask is whether the License Agreement will cover more than one type of property. If so, you need to make sure that the License Agreement is congruent with the underlying property's protective period. For example, if your License Agreement covers computer hardware and software, make sure that the hardware is licensed for 20 years (which is the length of the patent after GATT implementation), and the software is licensed for 70 years after death of author, if the copyright is based on a single author (which is the length of the copyright after GATT implementation). If the rights are for an area of technology susceptible to rapid changes, you need to decide if the licensee will be able to obtain an updated version if you make one.

Domestic License Clauses and Considerations

Recitals. Recitals identify the parties. The licensor is the property owner and the licensee is either the manufacturer or distributor.

Definitions. Definitions add clarity to the License Agreement. Copyrights, trademarks, patents, know-how, and other property that is to be licensed should be clearly defined to avoid confusion. Licensed products should be narrowly defined so as not to grant a license to one who cannot deliver certain goods subject of the license. For example, do not use the word "toy" to license one type of toy if the manufacturer has no ability to manufacture stuffed animals, dolls, etc. Other terms that should be defined include territory and royalty base.

License Grant. The grant is the essence of the License Agreement. It should define what type of license will be granted and what rights will be granted. For example, it may state that the license is exclusive in a patent for 5 years. If you grant an exclusive license, you should be specific as to whether you will retain any rights. You should state if there will be differing rights for different intellectual property, and whether the licensee will have the right to sublicense the property. If you allow assignment and sublicensing, make sure that you retain control.

Terms and Options. The licensor will generally want an initial short term and the licensee will seek adequate time to exploit the license. Options should be granted only if the licensee is in full compliance during the initial term.

Royalties. From a business perspective, royalties are the heart of the License Agreement. The licensor will need to determine price and payment terms, if he or she will want a flat fee, or royalty based on sales. The licensor will also need to decide how royalties will be paid.

For example, will they be paid on a fixed amount per item sold or on a percentage of sale basis? The licensor will also have to consider when royalties will be calculated and paid and if any minimum royalty should be imposed on the licensee. One of the most overlooked issues, and one of the most important, is to make sure to provide for accounting and auditing rights to determine if royalties are being paid as required.

Quality Control. The License Agreement should be drafted so the licensor has essentially strict quality control in saying how the license will be used. The quality control clauses should be buttressed by strong review and approval requirements. For example, in a Merchandising License Agreement, the manufacturer should be required to seek approval from the licensor at any preliminary and final stages, as well as first production approval. The licensor should also require that all trademark, patent numbers, and copyright symbols are prominently displayed on the licensed products. Lastly, the licensor should include a provision that failure to meet the quality control standards or properly mark the licensed products are grounds for termination.

Indemnification. The licensor may indemnify to third parties challenging the licensee's use of the property and the licensee may indemnify against false advertising, unfair competition by improper marketing, and selling defective products if the licensee is a manufacturer. The License Agreement should be drafted to provide the indemnifying party with the right to control litigation with counsel of own choice.

Exploitation by Licensee. This type of clause states when and how the licensee can market licensed products. It is important for the licensor to establish a starting date to protect against having to wait until end-of-term if the licensee does not start marketing/manufacturing the licensed products.

Termination. The license may expire at the end of the term or sooner by acts of either party. The licensor should draft the agreement to be able to terminate it upon the following conditions: 1) if the licensed product is recalled by the government; 2) if the licensee's actions damage or reflect adversely on the licensed property; 3) if the licensee repeatedly fails to make timely royalty payments;) generally, if the licensee attempts to assign or sublet his or her rights; and 5) where the licensee goes ahead without approval from the licensor, when approval was required.

International Licensing

Territory. Licensors should be aware of cross-collateralization (treating multiple territories as one for computing royalties). For example, if Italy, Germany, and Spain are added together to meet minimum royalty guarantees, the License Agreement allows for cross-collateralization and the licensor will get paid less on royalties than if each country has to meet minimum guarantees separately.

Ownership. International laws may render certain assignment language void, even if such language is okay in the United States.

Moral rights. Authors have certain rights that are not emphasized in the United States, but are highly emphasized in other countries. Such rights are called moral rights and include the right to have or not have the author's name on the art and the right to prevent mutilation of the author's works.

Taxes. Many foreign countries have tax laws designed to reduce licensor's gross revenues, so the licensor must be careful.

Royalty rates. The same issues that occur in domestic licenses apply to international agreements. Additionally, currency conversion and point of collection matters should be clearly discussed and defined.

Governing law. U.S. licensors should include clauses in their License Agreements so that the license is governed by U.S. law, and all conflicts are resolved by U.S. law.

Counterfeit and Gray Market Goods

Counterfeiting activity has flourished recently, due in part to newly industrialized nations acquiring the know-how and capability to mass-produce goods. Instead of using these new talents and resources to produce their own products, some foreign companies are turning their attention to the lucrative activity of selling counterfeit goods. Frequently, these goods are inferior; but even if not, counterfeit products steal profits from the rightful owner by offering lower prices to the owner's customers. Counterfeiters can do this because they piggy-back on the owner's goodwill without spending a cent on advertising, research and development, licensing, or marketing.

Unlike counterfeit goods (which are also known as black market goods), gray market goods bear a valid trademark or copyright associated with the goods. Gray market goods are foreign manufactured and are imported into the United States without consent of the United States trademark or copyright holder. Gray market activity has also exploded in recent years, due in part to developing countries' reluctance to enact or enforce laws mandating stricter guidelines for their exporting practices. The reason for this is simple: a reduction in exporting hinders the export country's economy.

Most recently, counterfeit and gray market industries have become multibillion dollar industries. With the pace of developments in multinational arrangements and the boom of counterfeit and gray market transactions, owners and manufacturers of domestic goods need to be aware of the steps that they can take to protect their name and products.

Trademark and copyright owners should use both the copyright and trademark systems to enhance protection for their products and intellectual property rights. If they do not register their trademarks and copyrights, they face one of the biggest obstacles of full protection for their products and product names: they will not be able to use certain trademark or copyright laws to enjoin illegal imports.

Additionally, trademark owners who sell abroad should consider international registration of their marks.

United States Customs Service

United States trademark and copyright laws give the United States Customs Service (Customs) authority to stop attempted entry of illegal imports. To seek protection with Customs, owners of registered trademarks, trade names, and copyrights need only notify and register their marks, names, or works with Customs (although registration is not automatic and Customs has the right to disapprove registration if any claim, rebuttal, or other relevant evidence weighs against registration). Once products are registered, Customs peruses incoming goods and restricts entry of goods that compare to domestic registered goods. If Customs declares the goods to be counterfeit, the goods are seized and the importer is given 30 days to contest the forfeiture. Unless the importer obtains written consent from the rightful owner to allow entry of the goods, it is virtually impossible for the goods to gain entry into the United States.

If the incoming products are considered gray market goods, Customs will detain the goods and give the importer 30 days to contest seizure and forfeiture. However, in this situation, both seizure and forfeiture may be avoided by the importer's unilateral invocation of uncontested entry of the goods as is, or entry of the goods with the counterfeit mark obliterated. Thus, although Customs is not a comprehensive solution to all illegal import problems, it has proven effective, and in some cases, very potent against such illegal activities.

United States International Trade Commission

One mechanism typically not known to the general public to protect themselves from illegal imports is to bring an action before the United States International Trade Commission. This commission receives formal complaints, reviews the complaints, and determines whether to launch a full-scale investigation. If the Commission finds a violation, it can exclude the illegal imports and order a cease and desist order against the persons involved in these activities. Two major benefits of bringing an action before the Commission are that the process is relatively quick and final decisions are appealable to the United States Court of Appeals. However, the major disadvantage is that monetary damages are not available. (Nevertheless, it may be possible for the owner to file a simultaneous action for monetary damages in the Federal District Court.)

Multinational Agreements

In addition to exerting pressure upon other nations to enact and enforce laws to prevent the export of counterfeit goods, the United States is entering into various multinational agreements designed to set minimum standards for trademark and other intellectual property protection. Some of the agreements include the General Agreement on Tariffs and Trade (GATT), the North American Free Trade Agreement (NAFTA), the Madrid Protocol, Community Trademark Regulation, and Trademark Law Treaty.

GATT

The General Agreement on Tariffs and Trade (GATT) began in 1986 and concluded at the end of 1993. GATT is the key multinational treaty set up to protect free trade among nations. In 1994, the United States, the European Union, and over 100 other countries signed the GATT agreement on Trade Related Aspects of Intellectual Property Rights (TRIPs). The GATT/TRIPs agreement requires all member nations to implement certain minimum standards for intellectual property violations at the border. One minimum standard is that member nations must grant the same protection to nationals of other member nations as it grants to its own nationals. This is known as "national treatment" and will help enhance harmony in international trademark affairs. TRIPs also requires member nations to provide a system for registration of trademarks and reasonable opportunity for petitions to cancel registrations that are suspect.

NAFTA

An agreement that became effective January 1, 1994 is the North American Free Trade Agreement (NAFTA). NAFTA is an agreement entered into by the United States, Canada, and Mexico to provide trade regulations between the three countries. Although NAFTA has been criticized for treading lightly in certain areas that one or another party has traditionally been reluctant to change, the trademark aspects of NAFTA are probably the least controversial. This may be due in part to the fact that the trademark provisions of NAFTA are patterned after the TRIPs agreement, and as such has similar provisions. For example, like TRIPs, NAFTA provides for national treatment and sets forth minimum standards to protect intellectual property by requiring mandatory provisions for border relief for trademark counterfeit goods. NAFTA also requires each member country to provide a system for registration that includes provisions for interested persons adversely affected by the registration of a mark to petition to cancel that registration.

Madrid Protocol

One agreement that will tremendously benefit U.S. trademark owners is the Madrid Protocol. This agreement supplements the long-standing Madrid Agreement that was adopted a century ago, but was deficient in matters important to the United States. The Madrid Protocol will clear up these deficiencies and will enable U.S. trademark owners to obtain international trademark registrations in one basic filing. The U.S. has supported the substantive provisions of this agreement, but for political reasons, the Clinton Administration withdrew support in May of 1994. Nevertheless, later that summer, Congress moved forward with legislation to implement U.S. accession to the Madrid Protocol subject to satisfactory resolution of the political issues.

Community Trademark Regulation

In March 1994, the trademark law in Europe, known as the Community Trademark Regulation, was enacted. This regulation enables a trademark owner the opportunity to file a single application to obtain trademark protection throughout the European Union. At first glance, one might think that this regulation only benefits the countries in Europe. However, any trademark owner in any country which participated in the Paris Convention will be able to file an application to obtain a Community Trademark. Thus, since the United States was a party to the Paris Convention, U.S. owners benefit by the Community Trademark Regulation. Once up and running, it is thought that the Community Trademark System will be linked to the Madrid Protocol.

Trademark Law Treaty

The United States has been involved in a diplomatic conference to conclude a treaty designed to deal with the procedural and administrative aspects of procuring, transferring, and renewing trademark rights. This treaty is known as the Trademark Law Treaty (TLT) and is the product of the World Intellectual Property Organization's (WIPO) efforts to harmonize international trademark procedures. The TLT will come into force after five member countries have signed, and as a supporter of this treaty, the United States is expected to be one of the signatories.

Part IV

Franchising

Why read about entering into a franchise agreement? Well, after being in business for awhile, you may grow so much that you decide to franchise *your* business. Then would you have wished you had read this chapter? You bet you would have! It offers tips on what a franchisee may ask of you, so why not be prepared? Thinking along the lines of becoming a franchisor is an example of the fourth key to a successful business: *to have vision.* You need to concentrate on the present but be prepared for the future. Those who have vision get ahead. Why? Because they prepare for the future and take concrete steps toward making their goals happen.

When they reach their present destination, some people call them lucky, and sometimes they are. However, more often than not they have carved their niche in life very strategically. They don't just work hard; most people work hard. They work smart. They have concrete goals at all stages in business and they carefully calculate strategic ways for meeting their goals. So when you read this chapter, do so with the vision that some day you will be a franchisor, your name will be known throughout the country, and your product will be a common household word. In this section, you will learn the following:

- The definition of a franchise.
- What to look for in a franchise/franchisor.
- Sources for locating a franchise.
- The legal aspects: The Disclosure Document and Franchise Agreement.

Locating and Evaluating a Franchise

A franchise is defined as a situation where the owner of particular goods or services allows a person or entity the legal right to market the owner's goods or services under certain standards in exchange for payment of a franchise fee. The owner is called the "franchisor" and the person or entity acquiring the rights is known as the "franchisee."

Sources for Locating a Franchise

Besides the sources listed in Chapter Two for purchasing a business, the following will provide assistance on locating a franchise:

1) The semi-annual publication of the International Franchise Association's *Franchise Opportunities Guide.*
2) *Franchise Opportunity Handbook* published by the U.S. Department of Commerce.
3) The quarterly publication of Enterprise Magazine's, *Inc's Franchise Handbook.*
4) The franchisor or his or her agent.
5) The Small Business Administration.
6) Franchising trade shows.
7) The section on franchise opportunities in your local library.

What to Look for in a Franchisor

The following questions should be asked when evaluating a franchisor:

1) Who is the franchisor?
2) How long has the franchisor been in business?
3) Who are the principal management people?
4) What is their background?
5) How long have they been with the franchisor?
6) What experience did they bring with them to the franchise?
7) Is this experience congruent to their franchise responsibilities?
8) Has the franchisor or anyone in management ever been subject of legal action by law enforcement or regulatory agencies?
9) Does principal management demonstrate an indepth experience which is reflected in their track record?
10) Is the franchisor in good financial shape?
11) Is the franchise growing at a steady pace?

What Is the Franchisor's Reputation?

What is the franchisor's reputation among its franchisees? Does the franchisor come to the franchisees' assistance when needed? Did the franchisor advise franchisees to have an attorney take a look at the Franchise Agreement? Did you speak to existing franchisees? If so, how did they describe the franchisor? How many did you speak to? How long has each franchisee been with the franchise? What types of demands did they ask of the franchisor? Has the franchisor asked for your qualifications to see if you would be a good candidate as a franchisee? This may determine if he or she is interested in a long-term relationship.

Chapter **11**

The Legal Aspects of Franchising

There are two legal documents that the prospective franchisee must read and understand before he or she enters into a franchise situation. One is the Disclosure Document and the other is the Franchise Agreement. If the prospective business owner does not have the knowledge and experience in dealing with such matters, he or she should consult with a professional advisor who does, because franchising is a complicated business, and a difficult one to get out of once you sign on the dotted line.

The Disclosure Document

Every franchise is regulated by federal law, and depending on which state you live in, some are further regulated by state law. The Federal Trade Commission regulates franchises under federal law. To assist in preventing fraud and deception in franchised situations, the FTC requires every franchisor to prepare an extensive disclosure document which provides detailed information about the franchisor and the franchise. This Disclosure Document must be presented to all prospective franchisees either at their first personal meeting with the franchisor, or at least ten days before the franchisee is asked to sign a Franchise Agreement, whichever is first.

The Disclosure Document is required to disclose at least the following matters, and if it doesn't, you need to find out why:

1) Identity and history of the franchisor.
2) History, experience, and skill level of the people behind the franchisor.
3) Litigation and bankruptcy history of the franchisor.
4) Required fees and investment costs.
5) Required obligations and affiliations of the franchisee.
6) Financial statements of the franchisor and earnings claims, if the franchisor makes them, including percentage of existing franchises that have actually achieved the results claimed.
7) Length of time the franchise agreement will be in effect.
8) Termination, cancellation, and renewal terms of the franchise agreement.
9) Financing arrangements, if any.
10) Training and site assistance information.
11) Statistical information of the total number of current franchises, the number of franchises projected in the future, and the number of franchises terminated.
12) A list of the names and addresses of other franchisees.
13) A description of the extent to which franchisees must personally participate in the franchised business.

In addition to federal protection, many states have enacted a description of the extent to which laws requiring disclosure, and some states further require the franchisor to register its offering in that state if it is going to conduct business there. Some states which presently require registration include: California, Connecticut, Hawaii, Illinois, Indiana, Maryland, Michigan, Minnesota, New York, North Dakota, Oregon, Rhode Island, South Dakota, Texas, Virginia, Washington, and Wisconsin.

It is up to you as the prospective purchaser to take advantage of these requirements and thoroughly investigate the franchisor. If a franchisor fails to meet federal or state requirements, it will be subject to a stiff penalty. But it will be your loss if you enter into a Franchise Agreement without checking it out thoroughly.

The Franchise Agreement

The Franchise Agreement is a binding legal contract which typically includes some of the same information that the Disclosure Document offers. If its terms are incongruent to the Disclosure Document, something is wrong and you should find out why the two don't agree. A Franchise Agreement is not like a Partnership Agreement whereby two parties come together to develop an agreement which is fair to both parties. Rather, the Franchise Agreement is prepared by the franchisor, and as such, may be biased in favor of the franchisor. Thus, review the Franchise Agreement to make sure it accurately reflects the representations made by the franchisor.

Issues in the Franchise Agreement and Disclosure Document

How much does the franchise really cost? What is the total price of the franchise package? What is the initial franchise fee? What does this price include? Sometimes it includes sales commissions, initial training costs, site assistance, start-up assistance, general and administrative costs, and an amount which provides support costs during which royalties will not be adequate to give remuneration. Sometimes it also includes equipment, fixtures, furniture, and inventory. If it doesn't include some or all of the items mentioned, then what is it for and will you be required to pay for these items at a later date? How much of the initial franchise fee must be paid at the time of signing the agreement? How much can be carried on terms? What is the average working capital that is necessary? How much of the total franchise cost applies toward hard assets? goodwill? training? other services?

Name. The name of the franchised business is extremely important. If the name is not registered with the U.S. Patent and Trademark Office (PTO), you could be involved in a lawsuit later on if the franchisor's mark infringes on another registered trademark, and it will cost you in money or in being required to change the name. If the name is not registered, ask why. If the franchisor says that it has applied for registration, find out how far along it is in the process. If the franchisor states that the name is unregisterable, you should see if they plan to change the name. If not, expect litigation some time down the road.

Terms. What is the length of the term? Usually, the larger the investment, the longer the term (because the franchisor would not be able to get franchisees to invest a half a million for, let's say, a five year grant). Older Franchise Agreements were written for a term of 20 plus years. But today, if as the franchisee you could negotiate a 5 year franchise period with 3 renewal options, at your option, subject to signing the then current Franchise Agreement with current terms, you'd be getting a good deal. Whatever the term, can the Franchise Agreement be terminated at an earlier time? If so, under what conditions? Do you have the right to purchase the franchise business or assets in the event of termination? On what basis may the franchise be terminated on an earlier basis? If the franchised business is terminated early, what amount will be paid by the franchisor, if any? Will goodwill be included in the price paid? Do you have renewal rights? If so, under what terms? Under what circumstances might you not be allowed to renew? If you don't renew at the end of your term and decide to compete with the franchisor, you could end up in litigation. However, if the Franchise Agreement has a post-term covenant not to compete, it may be unenforceable in some states.

Adjacent Territory in Individual Franchise Agreements

A savvy franchisor will not give you an option for adjacent territory. If you want it, you'll probably need to put money up-front and have a scheduled open date in each territory.

Multiple Unit Agreements. An experienced franchisor will always include a performance clause which will force you to open a particular number of units on a scheduled basis. Make sure you can meet the requirements before you sign the agreement.

Location. A veteran franchisor will always require the right to approve the franchised site. Some franchisors will require that their name be on the lease and will sublet the space to you. This allows the franchisor to control the site. Others will take an assignment of the lease, and therefore, in the event the Franchise Agreement expires or terminates for any reason, or if you default in paying rent or royalties, it will be possible for the franchisor to take over the location. If you have an exclusive territory, is it clearly defined? Can company-owned stores be placed in the same territory? Can the territory be altered in the future?

Plans and Specifications. As the franchisee, you will have to conform to the franchisor's layouts, designs, equipment, etc. If architectural assistance is provided, find out who pays. If there is an assignment of the sign face to the franchisor in the agreement, the franchisor may have the right to remove the sign face if the agreement is terminated.

Suppliers. The franchisor cannot force you to purchase products from them unless the products are unique; otherwise they could be held in violation of antitrust laws. More than likely you will be allowed to purchase inventory and supplies from either the franchisor or an approved supplier. Whoever you purchase goods from, you need to determine if their costs are competitive with other products of similar value.

Training. Is training provided? If so, it may be loosely defined. You need to find out what training will be offered and who will pay. Check into whether you're entitled to follow-up training or training available on request after the initial training, and find out who'll pay costs for such training. Also, make sure to ask if trainers will be duly qualified.

Royalties. Today, more and more franchisors are requiring royalties to be collected weekly, not monthly. Find out if you must meet a quota, and if so, see if it's reasonable. Find out if when quotas aren't met, will the territory be reduced or lost? If quotas are not required, find out what standard the franchisor imposes to ensure that all franchisees meet required standards.

Advertising. Will there be advertising? If so, will you be obligated to participate? Is the advertising program nationwide, statewide, or local? Will advertising be spent on selling the products or looking for new franchisees? Has the franchisor committed itself to spending no less in advertising than the amounts it collects in advertising fees? Must the company-owned stores contribute to the advertising fund in the same terms as the franchisees? Make sure you read the Franchise Agreement to see the restrictions on advertising and how much you'll have to pay.

Maintenance, Repairs, and Refurbishing. You'll undoubtedly see a clause in the Franchise Agreement which will require you to refurbish your franchise. (This is because Kentucky Fried Chicken did not have such a clause in their agreements and it cost them a lot of money to persuade franchisees to upgrade, and other franchisors learned from KFC.)

Insurance. How much insurance will you need? Who gets insurance proceeds if a loss occurs? The franchisor may require that it be shown as an additional insured in the policy.

Transferability. If you decide to sell your franchised business, you'll probably need to obtain prior consent of the franchisor, and typically the franchisor will charge a fee of $5,000 to $10,000 for the transfer. (Typically, you can expect to sell your ongoing franchise for 2-3 times what your income is, plus the value of assets.) The franchisor may also require the right to approve the purchaser, and will condition the transfer on the new purchaser meeting the same terms and conditions that you met. Does the franchisor have the first right of refusal? Can you sell to another owner, partner, or family member without being required to obtain permission from the franchisor?

Termination and Default. It's very, very difficult to terminate a franchise, even if the Franchise Agreement is well written.

Part V

The Four Keys to a Successful Business: Revisited and Explained

In previous sections you were taught the four keys to a successful business. In this section you'll revisit those keys and expand your knowledge of them. After reading this chapter, you'll have the ability to envision yourself as an entrepreneur. You will see that you have the potential to be a successful entrepreneur and you will create what you didn't think was attainable. Excited? You should be. You have already found out the necessary tools and knowledge to fulfill your dream of owning a successful business. Now you are about to realize that you are in charge. So what are you waiting for? Let's get through this part so you can get into business. As you know, the four keys are as follows:

- Focus on formation.
- See the whole picture.
- Protect your backside.
- Have vision.

All you need to do is keep in mind the four keys that will help you to run a successful business, place yourself in the proper mindset, and you will be there—literally in your own business. If you have accomplished some of the tasks in earlier chapters, chances are that you are already, or will soon be in business.

First Key: Focus on Formation

The first key to a successful business is to *focus on formation*. You must *plan* on the form in which to operate a business. This is the essence of business growth. If you *plan* to form a sole proprietorship, you'll have the foundation for an effective sole proprietorship. If you haphazardly *fall into* a sole proprietorship, you may be surprised by tax consequences, lack of growth ability, etc. Moreover, you are likely to change the business entity to a partnership or corporation in a *very* short period of time. Likewise, if you *plan* to form a partnership or corporation, you'll spend valuable time and money on changing the business structure rather than on operating the business. If you purchase an existing business, you will not have a choice with your initial form; however, you can assess its form to determine if and when you should make changes to the structure.

Second Key: See the Whole Picture

The second key to a successful business is *seeing the whole picture* before you open the doors. That's right, you have to imagine everything *in detail*. For example, you must consider purchasing a telephone. Ask yourself, what system will best suit your needs? How many lines do you need? Do you need a facsimile line? Will you need a conference call option? Will you need a speaker phone? What about call waiting or call forwarding? The list of questions can go on and on and this is only one item.

Numerous questions must be asked and *answered* for each common business expense and task. If you see the whole picture and anticipate the future, you'll have a chance to survive when you get into business. If you fail to consider common expenses and tasks, you will fail to include them in your budget, and you will have less money in your budget when the items present themselves. Oh, don't worry. It is just a matter of time before ordinary items present themselves and become crises. Don't be caught off guard. See the whole picture before ordinary tasks and expenses make an untimely appearance.

Third Key: Protect Your Backside

The third key to a successful business is to *protect your backside*. Consider this scenario: Five years ago you started the business on a shoestring. You were the butcher, baker, and candlestick maker. You sweat out the first five years, and there were numerous times when you ate only peanut butter and jelly sandwiches. Today, you've grown into a multimillion dollar business. Sounds like you made it, right? Well, what if you're hit with a lawsuit over a contract that you entered into years before? What if you're told that you had to abandon your name because it infringed upon another trademark? What if you're hit with a tax lien? What will happen to your business now? The truth is that your business can be forced into bankruptcy overnight. Protect your backside so this won't happen to you. If you protect your backside, you'll survive where so many fail.

Fourth Key: Have Vision

The fourth key to a successful business is to *have vision*. So what is vision? Theoretically speaking, it is pretty much where we *choose* to be. If you envision yourself as a successful businessperson, you *will be* a successful businessperson. Conversely, if you allow outside forces to stifle your vision of success, it's more likely that you will fail. You need to have a positive mental attitude and you need to believe you have the power to control your life. When you have the ability to envision yourself as a successful entrepreneur, you will have the belief that stimulates you to become that successful entrepreneur. That's all there is to it. Through the power of your mind, you possess the capacity to draw yourself to complete the tasks necessary to become a successful entrepreneur. The journey awaits you if you decide to take the challenge. Good luck.

Entrepreneurial Assessment Questionnaire Comparison

Look back to your answers on the Entrepreneurial Assessment Questionnaire which opened this book to see how you compare with successful entrepreneurs. However, keep in mind that there is no single set of characteristics that every successful entrepreneur has, and even if your answers differ, you can be a successful entrepreneur.

Are you willing to invest a substantial portion of your net worth in the venture, including taking out a second mortgage on your house if necessary? More than any other characteristic, total commitment to success, including taking out a second mortgage, is a characteristic that many entrepreneurs share.

What major sacrifices have you made in your lifestyle, family circumstances, and your standard of living to make progress in a previous situation? If you have not made any major sacrifices in your life, you do not know if you will be able to meet the demanding and stressful pressures of lack of money and lack of time that starting a business entails.

Are you driven internally by a strong desire to compete? Successful entrepreneurs are driven internally by a strong desire to compete and outperform others.

Would you like to outperform against your previous results or against a competitor? Entrepreneurs focus competition on themselves over their competitors. They set standards for themselves, strive to meet those standards, and when they do, they set higher ones and keep the process moving almost indefinitely.

Do you have a need to achieve? Successful entrepreneurs have a strong need to constantly achieve their highest potential.

Do you set goals? Successful entrepreneurs are goal-oriented. They set goals and focus on reaching them. Having such goals helps them to set the directions that they will go.

Have you ever willingly placed yourself in a situation where you were personally responsible for the success or failure of an operation? There is substantial evidence that entrepreneurs volunteer and take initiative, and thereby make themselves responsible for making things happen. They take responsibility for their actions and the actions of others.

Are you intimidated by certain people or situations? Entrepreneurs are not stopped by difficult people or situations. Business situations do not intimidate them. Rather, they are challenged by the most difficult situations and people.

Do you have a sense of humor? The most successful entrepreneurs can laugh at themselves and most situations.

Do you have a need to know how you are performing? Entrepreneurs who are on the move want recognition for their efforts. They want feedback on how well they are performing.

Do you like constant change or would you prefer a routine? The best entrepreneurs have a tolerance for ambiguity, stress, and uncertainty. They are generally flexible and have an attitude that tomorrow always comes.

Are you thinking about retirement? Entrepreneurs never seem to talk about retiring.

Are you a gambler or would you parachute out of an airplane? Most entrepreneurs are calculated risk takers, not gamblers.

Are you driven by a thirst for achievement or a thirst for status and power? Entrepreneurs have a tremendous need to achieve. Their need for status and power is low.

On a scale of 1-10, with 10 being the highest, how reliable are you? Studies show that entrepreneurs who are reliable are the most successful. Simply, that is the surest way to become a success.

On a scale of 1-10, with 10 being the highest, how much integrity do you have? Integrity is of utmost importance. If you do not have integrity, your chances to bind successful personal and business relationships will be nil. Eventually, everyone will find out your ethics and stay clear from you.

Do you have an urgent need to make decisions immediately? Entrepreneurs are quick decisions makers, yet they generally have a long-term view on how their decisions will fit in the whole picture.

Are you a visionary or would you rather stick with the facts at hand? The entrepreneur is both a visionary and one who sticks with the facts at hand.

In the past, how have you used failure as a way of learning? The best entrepreneurs use failure as a learning process to avoid similar problems in the future.

Do you have high energy? Entrepreneurs need to have lots of energy to deal with the long hours and stressful demands of entrepreneurial life.

How is your health? Entrepreneurs need to be quite healthy to endure the long days and stressful and sporadic situations.

Do you watch what you eat and drink? Many successful people watch what they eat and their sleeping habits because they know their good habits will help them be more productive. This is also true with successful entrepreneurs.

Do you exercise on a regular basis? Again, many successful people get themselves into exercise routines, whether it's a walking program, aerobics, sports, weight training, etc., and successful entrepreneurs are no exception.

Do you get away when you know you need some relaxation? Studies have shown that those who get away have more endurance and are in better spirits, and therefore more productive after they take some time for themselves. Successful entrepreneurs are no exception.

Would you consider yourself creative? The best entrepreneurs are either instinctually creative or they learn to be.

Do you believe you have high intelligence and conceptual abilities? Most entrepreneurs are conceptual, but intelligence levels vary.

State and Federal Agencies

Some government forms are included in this appendix. You can obtain those not included by contacting the government agency listed in this appendix for such forms. If you obtain and use all the necessary federal and state forms, you should be able to open the doors to your business with ease, knowing that you've done what's necessary to improve the chances of maintaining a successful business.

Federal Agencies: If you do not use the federal forms (federal employer identification number, employee tax forms, independent contractor tax forms, independent contractor factor form, and immigration form) contained in the forms section of this appendix, you can obtain such forms by contacting the following respective agency listed for each specific purpose:

INTERNAL REVENUE SERVICE	Federal Employer Identification Form IRS Form SS-4	Contact any IRS Office
	Independent Contractor Tax Form IRS Form 1099	Contact any IRS Office
	Independent Contractor Factors IRS Form SS-8	Contact any IRS Office
	Employee Tax Information Form IRS Form W-4	Contact any IRS Office
IMMIGRATION & NATURALIZATION SERVICE	Immigration Form I-9	Contact any INS Office
LIBRARY OF CONGRESS OFFICE	U.S. Copyright Application Forms	Register of Copyrights Library of Congress Washington, DC 20059

U.S PATENT & TRADEMARK OFFICE	U.S. Federal Trademark Applications	U.S. Dept. of Commerce Patent & Trademark Office Washington, DC 20231
	U.S. Patent Application	U.S. Dept. of Commerce Patent & Trademark Office Washington, DC 20231

Telephone numbers of 50 State Agencies and the District of Columbia. Contact the agency listed below for incorporating and trademark information and forms for the state in which you plan to do business:

Alabama	(334) 242-5324 (Corporations)
	(334) 242-5325 (Trademarks)
Alaska	(907) 465-2530 (Corporations & Trademarks)
Arizona	(602) 542-3135 (Corporations)
	(602) 542-6187 (Trademarks)
Arkansas	(501) 682-3425 (Corporations)
	(501) 682-3405 (Trademarks)
California	(916) 657-5448 (Corporations)
	(916) 653-4984 (Trademarks)
Colorado	(303) 894-2251 (Corporations)
	(303) 894-2200 (Trademarks)
Connecticut	(203) 566-8570 (Corporations)
	(203) 566-1721 (Trademarks)
	(203) 556-3216 (Application Form Orders)
Delaware	(302) 739-4111 (Secretary of State)
	(302) 739-3073 (Corporations & Trademarks)
Dist. of Columbia	(202) 727-7278 (Corporations)
Florida	(904) 487-6052 (Corporations)
	(904) 487-6051 (Trademarks)
Georgia	(404) 656-2817 (Corporations & Trademarks)
Hawaii	(808) 586-2727 (General)
Idaho	(208) 334-2301 (Corporations)
	(208) 334-2300 (Trademarks)

Illinois	(217) 782-7880 (Corporations)
	(217) 524-0400 (Trademarks)
Indiana	(317) 232-6576 (Corporations)
	(317) 232-6540 (Trademarks)
Iowa	(515) 281-5204 (Secretary of State)
Kansas	(913) 296-4564 (Corporations)
	(913) 296-4565 (Trademarks)
Kentucky	(502) 564-2848 (Corporations & Trademarks)
Louisiana	(504) 922-1000 (Secretary of State)
	(504) 925-4704 (Corporations & Trademarks)
Maine	(207) 287-4195 (Corporations & Trademarks)
Maryland	(410) 225-1340 or 225-1330 (Corporations)
	(410) 974-5531 (Trademarks)
Massachusetts	(617) 727-2850 (Secretary of State)
	(617) 727-9640 (Corporations)
	(617) 727-8329 (Trademarks)
Michigan	(517) 322-1166 (Secretary of State)
	(517) 334-6302 (Corporations)
	(517) 334-8106 (Trademarks)
Minnesota	(612) 296-2803 (Secretary of State)
Mississippi	(601) 359-1333 (Secretary of State)
Missouri	(314) 340-7490 (Corporations & Trademarks)
Montana	(406) 444-3665 (Corporations & Trademarks)
Nebraska	(402) 471-4079 (Corporations & Trademarks)
Nevada	(702) 687-5203 (Secretary of State)
New Hampshire	(603) 271-3244 (Corporations & Trademarks)
New Jersey	(609) 984-1900 (Secretary of State)
	(609) 530-6431 (Corporations)
	(609) 530-6422 (Trademarks)
New Mexico	(505) 827-4509 (Corporations)
	(505) 827-3600 (Trademarks)
New York	(518) 473-2492 (Corporations)
	(518) 474-4770 (Trademarks)
North Carolina	(919) 733-4201 (Corporations)
	(919) 733-4129 (Trademarks)
North Dakota	(701) 328-4284 (Corporations)
Ohio	(614) 466-4980 (Secretary of State)
	(614) 466-3910 (Corporations)
	(614) 466-2295 (Trademarks)
Oklahoma	(405) 521-3911 (Secretary of State)

Oregon	(503) 986-2200 (Corporations)
	(503) 986-2228 (Trademarks)
Pennsylvania	(717) 787-1057 (Corporations & Trademarks)
Rhode Island	(401) 277-3040 (Secretary of State)
	(401) 277-3040 (Corporations)
	(401) 277-1487 (Trademarks)
South Carolina	Forms sold through Kitco (800) 351-1244
	(605) 773-4845 (Corporations)
	(605) 773-5666 (Trademarks)
South Dakota	(605) 773-4845 (Secretary of State)
	(605) 773-4845 (Corporations)
	(605) 773-5666 (Trademarks)
Tennessee	(615) 741-0537 (Secretary of State)
	(615) 741-0531 (Trademarks)
Texas	(512) 463-5555 (Corporations)
	(512) 463-5576 (Trademarks)
Utah	(801) 530-4849 (Corporations & Trademarks)
Vermont	(802) 828-2386 (Corporations)
	(802) 828-2387 (Trademarks)
Virginia	(804) 371-9733 (Corporations & Trademarks)
Washington	(360) 753-7115 (Corporations)
	(360) 753-7120 (Trademarks)
West Virginia	(304) 558-8000 (Corporations & Trademarks)
Wisconsin	(608) 266-3590 (Corporations)
	(608) 266-5653 (Trademarks)
Wyoming	(307) 777-7311 (Corporations & Trademarks)

Form Section of Appendix

The following section contains forms that should be reviewed before preparing your own forms for starting and maintaining your business. As mentioned throughout this book, these forms are designed for simple transactions. If your situation is complex, you should contact an attorney in your area to discuss your needs. (In many cases, the attorney will not charge for a limited consultation.)

Form Name	Form Number
Bylaws, Resolutions, Meeting Minutes	Forms 1.1-1.6
IRS Form 2553: Election of Subchapter "S" Status	Form 2
Articles of Organization of Limited Liability Company	Form 3
UCC-1: Standard Financing Statement	Form 4
UCC-3: Request for Information or Copies	Form 5
Sale of Assets Agreement	Form 6
Sale of Stock Agreement	Form 7
Fictitious Business Name Statement	Form 8
State Name Reservation	Form 9
IRS Form SS-4: Federal Employer Identification Number	Form 10
IRS Form SS-8: Independent Contractor Factors	Form 11
IRS Form W-4	Form 12
INS Form I-9: Employment Eligibility Verification	Form 13

Form 1.1

Bylaws of
[Corporate Name]

Article I: Shareholders

Section 1.1. *Annual Meetings*. An annual meeting of stockholders shall be held for the election of directors at such date, time and place, either within or without the State of _____, as may be designated by resolution of the Board of Directors from time to time. Any other proper business may be transacted at the annual meeting.

Section 1.2. *Special Meetings*. Special meetings of stockholders for any purpose or purposes may be called at any time by the Board of Directors, or by a committee of the Board of Directors which has been duly designated by the Board of Directors and whose powers and authority, as expressly provided in a resolution of the Board of Directors, include the power to call such meetings, but such special meetings may not be called by any other person or persons.

Section 1.3. *Notice of Meetings*. Whenever stockholders are required or permitted to take any action at a meeting, a written notice of the meeting shall be given which shall state the place, date and hour of the meeting, and, in the case of a special meeting, the purpose or purposes for which the meeting is called. Unless otherwise provided by law, the certificate of incorporation or these by-laws, the written notice of any meeting shall be given not less than ten (10) nor more than sixty (60) days before the date of the meeting to each stockholder entitled to vote at such meeting. If mailed, such notice shall be deemed to be given when deposited in the mail, postage prepaid, directed to the stockholder at his address as it appears on the records of the corporation.

Section 1.4. *Adjournments*. Any meeting of stockholders, annual or special, may adjourn from time to time to reconvene at the same or some other place, and notice need not be given of any such adjourned meeting if the time and place thereof are announced at the meeting at which the adjournment is taken. At the adjourned meeting the corporation may transact any business which might have been transacted at the original meeting. If the adjournment is for more than thirty (30) days, or if after the adjournment a new record date is fixed for the adjourned meeting, a notice of the adjourned meeting shall be given to each stockholder of record entitled to vote at the meeting.

Section 1.5. *Quorum*. Except as otherwise provided by law, the certificate of incorporation or these by-laws, at each meeting of stockholders the presence in person or by proxy of the holders of shares of stock having a majority of the votes which could be cast by the holders of all outstanding shares of stock entitled to vote at the meeting shall be necessary and sufficient to constitute a quorum. In the absence of a quorum, the stockholders so present may, by majority vote, adjourn the meeting from time to time in the manner provided in Section 1.4 of these by-laws until a quorum shall attend. Shares of its own stock belonging to the corporation or to another corporation, if a majority of the shares entitled to vote in the election of directors of such other corporation is held, directly or indirectly, by the corporation, shall neither be entitled to vote nor be counted for quorum purposes; provided, however, that the foregoing shall not limit the right of the corporation to vote stock, including but not limited to its own stock, held by it in a fiduciary capacity.

Section 1.6. *Organization*. Meetings of stockholders shall be presided over by the Chairman of the Board, if any, or in his absence by the Vice Chairman of the Board, if any, or in his absence by the President, or in his absence by a Vice President, or in the absence of the foregoing persons by a chairman designated by the Board of Directors, or in the absence of such designation by a chairman chosen at the meeting. The Secretary shall act as secretary of the meeting, but in his absence the chairman of the meeting may appoint any person to act as secretary of the meeting.

Section 1.7. *Voting; Proxies*. Except as otherwise provided by the certificate of incorporation, each stockholder entitled to vote at any meeting of stockholders shall be entitled to one vote for each share of stock held by him which has voting power upon the matter in question. Each stockholder entitled to vote at a meeting of stockholders may authorize another person or persons to act for him by proxy, but no such proxy shall be voted or acted upon after three (3) years from its date, unless the proxy provides for a longer period. A duly executed proxy shall be irrevocable if it states that it is irrevocable and if, and only as long as, it is coupled with an interest sufficient in law to support an irrevocable power. A stockholder may revoke any proxy which is not irrevocable by attending the meeting and voting in person or by filing an instrument in writing revoking the proxy or another duly executed proxy bearing a later date with the Secretary of the corporation. Voting at meetings of stockholders need not be by written ballot and need not be conducted by inspectors of election unless so determined by the holders of shares of stock having a majority of the votes which could be cast by the holders of all out-standing shares of stock entitled to vote thereon which are present in person or by proxy at such meeting. At all meetings of stockholders for the election of directors a plurality of the votes cast shall be sufficient to elect. All other elections and questions shall, unless otherwise provided by law, the certificate of incorporation or these bylaws, be decided by the vote of the holders of shares of stock having a majority of the votes which could be cast by the holders of all shares of stock entitled to vote thereon which are present in person or represented by proxy at the meeting.

Section 1.8. *Fixing Date for Determination of Stockholders of Record.* In order that the corporation may determine the stockholders entitled to notice of or to vote at any meeting of stockholders or any adjournment thereof, or to express consent to corporate action in writing without a meeting, or entitled to receive payment of any dividend or other distribution or allotment of any rights, or entitled to exercise any rights in respect of any change, conversion or exchange of stock or for the purpose of any other lawful action, the Board of Directors may fix a record date, which record date shall not precede the date upon which the resolution fixing the record date is adopted by the Board of Directors and which record date: (1) in the case of determination of stockholders entitled to vote at any meeting of stockholders or adjournment thereof, shall, unless otherwise required by law, not be more than sixty (60) nor less than ten (10) days before the date of such meeting; (2) in the case of determination of stockholders entitled to express consent to corporate action in writing without a meeting, shall not be more than ten (10) days from the date upon which the resolution fixing the record date is adopted by the Board of Directors: and (3) in the case of any other action, shall not be more than sixty (60) days prior to such other action. If no record date is fixed: (1) the record date for determining stockholders entitled to notice of or to vote at a

Appendix

meeting of stockholders shall be at the close of business on the day next preceding the day on which notice is given, or, if notice is waived, at the close of business on the day next preceding the day on which the meeting is held; (2) the record date for determining stockholders entitled to express consent to corporate action in writing without a meeting when no prior action of the Board of Directors is required by law, shall be the first date on which a signed written consent setting forth the action taken or proposed to be taken is delivered to the corporation in accordance with applicable law, or, if prior action by the Board of Directors is required by law, shall be at the close of business on the day on which the Board of Directors adopts the resolution taking such prior action; and (3) the record date for determining stockholders for any other purpose shall be at the close of business on the day on which the Board of Directors adopts the resolution relating thereto. A determination of stockholders of record entitled to notice of or to vote at a meeting of stockholders shall apply to any adjournment of the meeting; provided, however, that the Board of Directors may fix a new record date for the adjourned meeting.

Section 1.9. *List of Stockholders Entitled to Vote.* The Secretary shall prepare and make, at least ten (10) days before every meeting of stockholders, a complete list of the stockholders entitled to vote at the meeting, arranged in alphabetical order, and showing the address of each stockholder and the number of shares registered in the name of each stockholder. Such list shall be open to the examination of any stockholder, for any purpose germane to the meeting, during ordinary business hours, for a period of at least ten (10) days prior to the meeting, either at a place within the city where the meeting is to be held, which place shall be specified in the notice of the meeting, or, if not so specified, at the place where the meeting is to be held. The list shall also be produced and kept at the time and place of the meeting during the whole time thereof and may be inspected by any stockholder who is present. Upon the willful neglect or refusal of the directors to produce such a list at any meeting for the election of directors, they shall be ineligible for election to any office at such meeting. The stock ledger shall be the only evidence as to who are the stockholders entitled to examine the stock ledger, the list of stockholders or the books of the corporation, or to vote in person or by proxy at any meeting of stockholders.

Section 1.10. *Action by Consent of Stockholders.* Unless otherwise restricted by the certificate of incorporation, any action required or permitted to be taken at any annual or special meeting of the stockholders may be taken without a meeting, without prior notice and without a vote, if a consent in writing, setting forth the action so taken, shall be signed by the holders of outstanding stock having not less than the minimum number of votes that would be necessary to authorize or take such action at a meeting at which all shares entitled to vote thereon were present and voted. Prompt notice of the taking of the corporate action without a meeting by less than unanimous written consent shall be given to those stockholders who have not consented in writing.

Article II: Board of Directors

Section 2.1. *Number; Qualifications.* The Board of Directors shall consist of one or more members, the number thereof to be determined from time to time by resolution of the Board of Directors. Directors need not be stockholders.

Section 2.2. *Election; Resignation; Removal; Vacancies.* The Board of Directors shall initially consist of the persons named as directors in the Articles of incorporation, and each director so elected shall hold office until the first annual meeting of stockholders or until his successor is elected and qualified. At the first annual meeting of stockholders and at each annual meeting thereafter, the stockholders shall elect directors each of whom shall hold office for a term of one year or until his successor is elected and qualified. Any director may resign at any time upon written notice to the corporation. Any newly created directorship or any vacancy occurring in the Board of Directors for any cause may be filled by a majority of the remaining members of the Board of Directors, although such majority is less than a quorum, or by a plurality of the votes cast at a meeting of stockholders, and each director so elected shall hold office until the expiration of the tern of office of the director whom he has replaced or until his successor is elected and qualified.

Section 2.3. *Regular Meetings.* Regular meetings of the Board of Directors may be held at such places within or without the State of _____ and at such times as the Board of Directors may from time to time determine, and if so determined notices thereof need not be given.

Section 2.4. *Special Meetings*. Special meetings of the Board of Directors may be held at any time or place within or without the State of _____ whenever called by the President, any Vice President, the Secretary, or by any member of the Board of Directors. Notice of a special meeting of the Board of Directors shall be given by the person or persons calling the meeting at least twenty-four hours before the special meeting.

Section 2.5. *Telephonic Meetings Permitted*. Members of the Board of Directors, or any committee designated by the Board of Directors, may participate in a meeting thereof by means of conference telephone or similar communications equipment by means of which all persons participating in the meeting can hear each other, and participation in a meeting pursuant to this by-law shall constitute presence in person at such meeting.

Section 2.6. *Quorum; Vote Required for Action*. At all meetings of the Board of Directors a majority of the whole Board of Directors shall constitute a quorum for the transaction of business. Except in cases in which the certificate of incorporation or these by-laws otherwise provide, the vote of a majority of the directors present at a meeting at which a quorum is present shall be the act of the Board of Directors.

Section 2.7. *Organization*. Meetings of the Board of Directors shall be presided over by the Chairman of the Board, if any, or in his absence by the Vice Chairman of the Board, if any, or in his absence by the President, or in their absence by a chairman chosen at the meeting. The Secretary shall act as secretary of the meeting, but in his absence the chairman of the meeting may appoint any person to act as secretary of the meeting.

Section 2.8. *Informal Action by Directors*. Unless otherwise restricted by the certificate of incorporation or these by-laws, any action required or permitted to be taken at any meeting of the Board of Directors, or of any committee thereof, may be taken without a meeting if all members of the Board of Directors or such committee, as the case may be, consent thereto in writing, and the writing or writings are filed with the minutes of proceedings of the Board of Directors or such committee.

Article III: Officers

Section 3.1. *Executive Officers; Election; Qualifications; Term of Office; Resignation; Removal; Vacancies.* The Board of Directors shall elect a President and Secretary, and it may, if it so determines, choose a Chairman of the Board and a Vice Chairman of the Board from among its members. The Board of Directors may also choose one or more Vice Presidents, one or more Assistant Secretaries, a Treasurer and one or more Assistant Treasurers. Each such officer shall hold office until the first meeting of the Board of Directors after the annual meeting of stockholders next succeeding his election, and until his successor is elected and qualified or until his earlier resignation or removal. Any officer may resign at any time upon written notice to the corporation. The Board of Directors may remove any officer with or without cause at any time, but such removal shall be without prejudice to the contractual rights of such officer, if any, with the corporation. Any number of offices may be held by the same person. Any vacancy occurring in any office of the corporation by death, resignation, removal or otherwise may be filled for the unexpired portion of the term by the Board of Directors at any regular or special meeting.

Section 3.2. *Powers and Duties of Executive Officers.* The officers of the corporation shall have such powers and duties in the management of the corporation as may be prescribed by the Board of Directors and, to the extent not so provided, as generally pertain to their respective offices, subject to the control of the Board of Directors. The Board of Directors may require any officer, agent or employee to give security for the faithful performance of his duties.

Article IV: Stock

Section 4.1. *Certificates.* Every holder of stock shall be entitled to have a certificate signed by or in the name of the corporation by the Chairman or Vice Chairman of the Board of Directors, if any, or the President or a Vice President and by the Treasurer or an Assistant Treasurer, or the Secretary or an Assistant Secretary, of the corporation, certifying the number of shares owned by him in the corporation. Any of or all the signatures on the certificate may be a facsimile. In case any officer, transfer agent, or registrar who has signed or whose facsimile signature has been placed upon a certificate shall have ceased to be such officer. transfer agent, or registrar before such certificate is issued, it may be issued by the corporation with the same effect as if he were such officer, transfer agent, or registrar at the date of issue.

Section 4.2. *Loss, Stolen or Destroyed Stock Certificates; Issuance of New Certificates.* The corporation may issue a new certificate of stock in the place of any certificate theretofore issued by it, alleged to have been lost, stolen or destroyed. and the corporation may require the owner of the lost, stolen or destroyed certificate. or his legal representative, to give the corporation a bond sufficient to indemnify it against any claim that may be made against it any account of the alleged loss, theft or destruction of any such certificate or the issuance of such new certificate.

Article V: Indemnification

Section 5.1. *Right to Indemnification.* The corporation shall indemnify and hold harmless, to the fullest extent permitted by applicable law as it presently exists or may hereafter be amended, any person who was or is made or is threatened to be made a party or is otherwise involved in any action, suit or proceeding, whether civil, criminal, administrative or investigative (a proceeding) by reason of the fact that he, or a person for whom he hi the legal representative, is or was a director, officer, employee or agent of the corporation or is or was serving at the request of the corporation as a director, officer, employee or agent of another corporation or of a partnership, joint venture, trust, enterprise or non-profit entity, including service with respect to employee benefit plans, against all liability and loss suffered and expenses reasonably incurred by such person. The corporation shall be required to indemnify a person in connection with a proceeding initiated by such person only if the proceeding was authorized by the Board of Directors of the corporation.

Section 5.2. *Prepayment of Expenses.* The corporation shall pay the expenses incurred in defending any proceeding in advance of its final disposition, provided, however, that the payment of expenses incurred by a director or officer in advance of the final disposition of the proceeding shall be made only upon receipt of an undertaking by the director or officer to repay all amounts advanced if it should be ultimately determined that the director or officer is not entitled to be indemnified under this Article or otherwise.

Section 5.3. *Claims.* If a claim for indemnification or payment of expenses under this Article is not paid in full within sixty days after a written claim therefor has been received by the corporation the claimant may file suit to recover the unpaid amount of such claim and, if successful in whole or in part, shall be entitled to be paid the expense of prosecuting such claim. In any such action the corporation shall have the burden of proving that the claimant was not entitled to the requested indemnification or payment of expenses under applicable law.

Section 5.4. *Non-Exclusivity of Rights.* The rights conferred on any person by this Article VI shall not be exclusive of any other rights which such person may have or hereafter acquire under any statute, provision of the certificate of incorporation, these by-laws, agreement, vote of stockholders or disinterested directors or otherwise.

Section 5.5. *Other Indemnification.* The corporation's obligation, if any, to indemnify any person who was or is serving at its request as a director, officer, employee or agent of another corporation, partnership, joint venture, trust, enterprise or non-profit entity shall be reduced by any amount such person may collect as indemnification from such other corporation, partnership, joint venture, trust, enterprise or non-profit enterprise.

Section 5.6. *Amendment or Repeal.* Any repeal or modification of the foregoing provisions of this Article Vl shall not adversely affect any right or protection hereunder of any person in respect of any act or omission occurring prior to the time of such repeal or modification.

Article VI: Miscellaneous

Section 6.1. *Fiscal Year.* The fiscal year of the corporation shall be determined by resolution of the Board of Directors.

Section 6.2. *Seal.* The corporate seal shall have the name of the corporation inscribed thereon and shall be in such form as may be approved from time to time by the Directors.

Section 6.3. *Waiver of Notice of Meetings of Stockholders and Directors.* Any written waiver of notice, signed by the person entitled to notice, whether before or after the time stated therein, shall be deemed equivalent to notice. Attendance of a person at a meeting shall constitute a waiver of notice of such meeting, except when the person attends a meeting for the express purpose of objecting, at the beginning of the meeting, to the transaction of any business because the meeting is not lawfully called or convened. Neither the business to be transacted at, nor the purpose of any regular or special meeting of the stockholders, directors, or members of a committee of directors need be specified in any written waiver of notice.

Section 6.4. *Interested Directors; Quorum.* No contract or transaction between the corporation and one or more of its directors or officers, or between the corporation and any other corporation, partnership, association, or other organization in which one or more of its directors or officers are directors or officers, or have a financial interest, shall be void or voidable solely for this reason, or solely because the director or officer is present at or participates in the meeting of the Board of Directors or committee thereof which authorizes the contract or transaction, or solely because his or their votes are counted for such purpose, if: (I) the material facts as to his relationship or interest and as to the contract or transaction are disclosed or are known to the Board of Directors or the committee, and the Board of Directors or committee in good faith authorizes the contract or transaction by the affirmative votes of a majority of the disinterested directors, even though the disinterested directors be less than a quorum; or (2) the material facts as to his relationship or interest and as to the contract or transaction are disclosed or are known to the stockholders entitled to vote thereon, and the contract or transaction is specifically approved in good faith by vote of the stockholders; or (3) the contract or transaction is fair as to the corporation as of the time it is authorized, approved or ratified, by the Board of Directors, a committee thereof, or the stockholders. Common or interested directors may be counted in determining the presence of a quorum at a meeting of the Board of Directors or of a committee which authorizes the contract or transaction.

Section 6.5. *Amendment of By-Laws.* These by-laws may be altered or repealed, and new by-laws made, by the Board of Directors, but the stockholders may make additional by-laws and may alter and repeal any by-laws whether adopted by them or otherwise.

Certificate of Secretary

I, the undersigned, do hereby certify as follows: I am the present duly elected and acting Secretary of the above named corporation, under the laws of the State of _____; and the foregoing Bylaws constitute the original Bylaws of said corporation as duly adopted by the incorporator on ___ day of _____, 199___.

IN WITNESS WHEREOF, I have subscribed my name and affixed the seal of this Corporation on the ___ day of _____, 199___.

_____
Secretary

Form 1.2

Resolution by Joint Written Consent of Board of Directors and Shareholders
of
[Name of Corporation]

The undersigned, being [all of the directors OR the sole director] of [name of corporation], (the "Corporation") and all of the shareholders of the Corporation, in accordance with the authority contained in the laws of the State of [Incorporation] and the Bylaws of this Corporation, do hereby consent to the adoption of the following recitals and resolutions:

RESOLUTION TO [STATE PURPOSE]

WHEREAS, it is deemed to be advisable and in the best interests of this Corporation and its shareholders that the ... be approved and adopted;

NOW THEREFORE BE IT RESOLVED, that the ... be, and in all respects it hereby is, approved and adopted.

IN WITNESS WHEREOF, the undersigned, as [all of the directors OR the sole director] of [name of corporation], have/has executed this Action by Written Consent as of this _____ day of _____.

_____

Name, Director

IN WITNESS WHEREOF, the undersigned, as holders of all of the issued and outstanding shares of capital stock of the Corporation, hereby consent to the adoption of the foregoing recitals and resolutions and approve, adopt, ratify, and confirm the, and execute this Action by Written Consent as of this _____ day of _____

_____

Name, Shareholder

Form 1.3

Waiver of Notice and Consent to Hold [Regular/Special] Meeting of Board of Directors of [Name of Corporation]

We, the undersigned, being all the Directors of the Corporation hereby agree and consent that the [annual/special] meeting of the Board of Directors of the Corporation be held on the date and time, and at the place designated hereunder, and do hereby waive all notice whatsoever of such meeting and of any adjournment or adjournments thereof.

We do further agree and consent that any and all lawful business may be transacted at such meeting, or at any adjournment or adjournments thereof, as may be deemed advisable by the Directors present thereat. Any business transacted at such meeting or at any adjournment or adjournments thereof, shall be as valid and legal and of the same force and effect as if such meeting or adjourned meeting were held after notice.

Place of Meeting: _____

Date of Meeting: _____

Time of Meeting: _____

Dated: _____

_____

Director

_____

Director

Form 1.4

Minutes of [Regular/Special]
Meeting of Shareholders
of
[Name of Corporation]

A[n] [annual/special] meeting of the Shareholders of the above Corporation was held on the date, time and at the place set forth in the written Waiver of Notice signed by the Shareholders, fixing such time and place, and prefixed to the Minutes of this meeting.

The following Shareholders were present at the meeting, in person or by proxy, representing shares as indicated: [List Shareholders]

The President of the Corporation called the meeting to order and announced that the meeting was held pursuant to waiver of notice and written consent to the holding of the meeting and, on a motion duly made, seconded, and unanimously carried, was made a part of the records and ordered inserted in the minute book immediately preceding the records of this meeting.

The minutes of the previous meeting of Shareholders were then read and approved. It was then moved, seconded, and unanimously resolved to dispense with the reading of the minutes of the last meeting.

The President announced that the next order of business was the election of Directors, to serve until the next annual meeting of shareholders, and until their successors have been duly elected and qualified.

The following nominations were made and seconded: [Names of Proposed Directors]

The President then announced that the next order of business was approval by the Shareholders of _____. After discussion, the matter was [approved/disapproved] by the Shareholders by the following vote:_____

The President then announced that the last order of business was approval and ratification by the Shareholders of the actions of Directors and Officers of the Corporation occurring between the last annual meeting and this meeting. After discussion, the matter was [approved/disapproved] by the Shareholders by the following vote:_____

There being no further business to come before the meeting, on motion duly made, seconded, and adopted, the meeting was adjourned.

_____

Secretary

_____

Shareholder

Form 1.5

Waiver of Notice and Consent to Hold
[Annual/Special] Meeting of Shareholders
of
[Name of Corporation]

We, the undersigned, being all of the Shareholders of the Corporation hereby agree and consent that the [Annual/Special] meeting of the Shareholders of the Corporation be held on the date and time, and at the place designated hereunder, and do hereby waive all notice whatsoever of such meeting and of any adjournment or adjournments thereof.

We do further agree and consent that any and all lawful business may be transacted at such meeting, or at any adjournment or adjournments thereof, as may be deemed advisable by the Directors present thereat. Any business transacted at such meeting or at any adjournment or adjournments thereof, shall be as valid and legal and of the same force and effect as if such meeting or adjourned meeting were held after notice was duly given.

Place of Meeting: _____

Date of Meeting: _____

Time of Meeting: _____

Dated: _____

_____
Shareholder

_____
Shareholder

Appendix

Form 1.6

Minutes of [Regular/Special] Meeting of Board of Directors of [Name of Corporation]

A [regular/special] meeting of the Board of Directors of the above captioned Corporation was held on the date, time, and at the place set forth in the written Waiver of Notice signed by the directors, fixing such time and place, and prefixed to the Minutes of this meeting.

The following Directors were present at the meeting:

The following individuals also were present at the meeting:

The Chairman called the meeting to order and announced that the meeting was held pursuant to written waiver of notice and consent to the holding of the meeting. The waiver and consent was presented to the meeting and, on a motion duly made, seconded, and carried, was made a part of the records and ordered inserted in the minute book immediately preceding the records of this meeting.

The minutes of the last meeting of Directors were then read and approved. It was then moved, seconded, and resolved to dispense with the reading of the minutes of the last meeting.

The Chairman stated that the election of new officers was in order. The board then proceeded to elect new officers of the Corporation. The following nominations were made and seconded:

Name	Office
_____	President
_____	Vice President
_____	Secretary
_____	Chief Financial Officer/Treasurer

No further nominations were made, and the persons named above were duly elected to the offices set forth opposite their respective names.

The Chairman then announced that the last order of business was approval and ratification by the Board of Directors of the actions of Directors and Officers of the Corporation occurring between the last meeting and this meeting. After discussion and on a motion duly made, seconded, and carried, the board approved and ratified the actions of Directors and Officers of the Corporation.

There being no further business to come before the meeting, the meeting was duly adjourned.

_____

Secretary

_____

Director

_____

Director

Form 2

IRS Form 2553: Election of Subchapter S Status with Instructions

---

Form **2553** Department of the Treasury Internal Revenue Service	**Election by a Small Business Corporation** (Under section 1362 of the Internal Revenue Code) ▶ For Paperwork Reduction Act Notice, see page 1 of instructions. ▶ See separate instructions.	OMB No. 1545-0146

Notes: 1. This election, to be an "S corporation," can be accepted only if all the tests are met under **Who May Elect** on page 1 of the instructions; all signatures in Parts I and III are originals (no photocopies); and the exact name and address of the corporation and other required form information are provided.

2. Do not file **Form 1120S,** U.S. Income Tax Return for an S Corporation, until you are notified that your election is accepted.

Part I	**Election Information**		
Please Type or Print	Name of corporation (see instructions)	**A** Employer identification number (EIN)	
	Number, street, and room or suite no. (If a P.O. box, see instructions.)	**B** Date incorporated	
	City or town, state, and ZIP code	**C** State of incorporation	

D Election is to be effective for tax year beginning (month, day, year) . . . . ▶ / /

E Name and title of officer or legal representative who the IRS may call for more information

F Telephone number of officer or legal representative (   )

G If the corporation changed its name or address after applying for the EIN shown in **A,** check this box . . . . ▶ ☐

H If this election takes effect for the first tax year the corporation exists, enter month, day, and year of the **earliest** of the following: (1) date the corporation first had shareholders, (2) date the corporation first had assets, or (3) date the corporation began doing business . . . . ▶ / /

I Selected tax year: Annual return will be filed for tax year ending (month and day) ▶ ....

If the tax year ends on any date other than December 31, except for an automatic 52-53-week tax year ending with reference to the month of December, you **must** complete Part II on the back. If the date you enter is the ending date of an automatic 52-53-week tax year, write "52-53-week year" to the right of the date. See Temporary Regulations section 1.441-2T(e)(3).

J Name and address of each shareholder, shareholder's spouse having a community property interest in the corporation's stock, and each tenant in common, joint tenant, and tenant by the entirety. (A husband and wife (and their estates) are counted as one shareholder in determining the number of shareholders without regard to the manner in which the stock is owned.)	**K** Shareholders' Consent Statement. Under penalties of perjury, we declare that we consent to the election of the above-named corporation to be an "S corporation" under section 1362(a) and that we have examined this consent statement, including accompanying schedules and statements, and to the best of our knowledge and belief, it is true, correct, and complete. (Shareholders sign and date below.)*		**L** Stock owned		**M** Social security number or employer identification number (see instructions)	**N** Shareholder's tax year ends (month and day)
	Signature	Date	Number of shares	Dates acquired		

*For this election to be valid, the consent of each shareholder, shareholder's spouse having a community property interest in the corporation's stock, and each tenant in common, joint tenant, and tenant by the entirety must either appear above or be attached to this form. (See instructions for Column K if a continuation sheet or a separate consent statement is needed.)

Under penalties of perjury, I declare that I have examined this election, including accompanying schedules and statements, and to the best of my knowledge and belief, it is true, correct, and complete.

Signature of officer ▶   **Title** ▶   **Date** ▶

See Parts II and III on back.   Form **2553**

*Government forms may vary each year. Consult your current year's forms for complete information.

Form 2

IRS Form 2553: Election of Subchapter S Status with Instructions (continued)

Form 2553   Page **2**

Part II — Selection of Fiscal Tax Year (All corporations using this part must complete item O and one of items P, Q, or R.)

O   Check the applicable box below to indicate whether the corporation is:

    1. ☐ A new corporation adopting the tax year entered in item I, Part I.

    2. ☐ An existing corporation retaining the tax year entered in item I, Part I.

    3. ☐ An existing corporation changing to the tax year entered in item I, Part I.

P   Complete item P if the corporation is using the expeditious approval provisions of Revenue Procedure 87-32, 1987-2 C.B. 396, to request: **(1)** a natural business year (as defined in section 4.01(1) of Rev. Proc. 87-32), or **(2)** a year that satisfies the ownership tax year test in section 4.01(2) of Rev. Proc. 87-32. Check the applicable box below to indicate the representation statement the corporation is making as required under section 4 of Rev. Proc. 87-32.

    1. Natural Business Year ► ☐ I represent that the corporation is retaining or changing to a tax year that coincides with its natural business year as defined in section 4.01(1) of Rev. Proc. 87-32 and as verified by its satisfaction of the requirements of section 4.02(1) of Rev. Proc. 87-32. In addition, if the corporation is changing to a natural business year as defined in section 4.01(1), I further represent that such tax year results in less deferral of income to the owners than the corporation's present tax year. I also represent that the corporation is not described in section 3.01(2) of Rev. Proc. 87-32. (See instructions for additional information that must be attached.)

    2. Ownership Tax Year ► ☐ I represent that shareholders holding more than half of the shares of the stock (as of the first day of the tax year to which the request relates) of the corporation have the same tax year or are concurrently changing to the tax year that the corporation adopts, retains, or changes to per item I, Part I. I also represent that the corporation is not described in section 3.01(2) of Rev. Proc. 87-32.

Note: If you do not use item P and the corporation wants a fiscal tax year, complete either item Q or R below. Item Q is used to request a fiscal tax year based on a business purpose and to make a back-up section 444 election. Item R is used to make a regular section 444 election.

Q   Business Purpose—To request a fiscal tax year based on a business purpose, you must check box Q1 and pay a user fee. See instructions for details. You may also check box Q2 and/or box Q3.

    1. Check here ► ☐ if the fiscal year entered in item I, Part I, is requested under the provisions of section 6.03 of Rev. Proc. 87-32. Attach to Form 2553 a statement showing the business purpose for the requested fiscal year. See instructions for additional information that must be attached.

    2. Check here ► ☐ to show that the corporation intends to make a back-up section 444 election in the event the corporation's business purpose request is not approved by the IRS. (See instructions for more information.)

    3. Check here ► ☐ to show that the corporation agrees to adopt or change to a tax year ending December 31 if necessary for the IRS to accept this election for S corporation status in the event: (1) the corporation's business purpose request is not approved and the corporation makes a back-up section 444 election, but is ultimately not qualified to make a section 444 election, or (2) the corporation's business purpose request is not approved and the corporation did not make a back-up section 444 election.

R   Section 444 Election—To make a section 444 election, you must check box R1 and you may also check box R2.

    1. Check here ► ☐ to show the corporation will make, if qualified, a section 444 election to have the fiscal tax year shown in item I, Part I. To make the election, you must complete **Form 8716**, Election To Have a Tax Year Other Than a Required Tax Year, and either attach it to Form 2553 or file it separately.

    2. Check here ► ☐ to show that the corporation agrees to adopt or change to a tax year ending December 31 if necessary for the IRS to accept this election for S corporation status in the event the corporation is ultimately not qualified to make a section 444 election.

Part III — Qualified Subchapter S Trust (QSST) Election Under Section 1361(d)(2)**

Income beneficiary's name and address	Social security number
Trust's name and address	Employer identification number

Date on which stock of the corporation was transferred to the trust (month, day, year) . . . . ►   /   /

In order for the trust named above to be a QSST and thus a qualifying shareholder of the S corporation for which this Form 2553 is filed, I hereby make the election under section 1361(d)(2). Under penalties of perjury, I certify that the trust meets the definitional requirements of section 1361(d)(3) and that all other information provided in Part III is true, correct, and complete.

_____   _____

Signature of income beneficiary or signature and title of legal representative or other qualified person making the election   Date

**Use of Part III to make the QSST election may be made only if stock of the corporation has been transferred to the trust on or before the date on which the corporation makes its election to be an S corporation. The QSST election must be made and filed separately if stock of the corporation is transferred to the trust after the date on which the corporation makes the S election.

*U.S. Government Printing Office: 1993 — 301-628/80271

---

*Government forms may vary each year. Consult your current year's forms for complete information.

Form 2

IRS Form 2553: Election of Subchapter S Status with Instructions (continued)

Department of the Treasury
Internal Revenue Service

Instructions for Form 2553
(Revised September 19   )
Election by a Small Business Corporation
Section references are to the Internal Revenue Code unless otherwise noted.

Paperwork Reduction Act Notice.—We ask for the information on this form to carry out the Internal Revenue laws of the United States. You are required to give us the information. We need it to ensure that you are complying with these laws and to allow us to figure and collect the right amount of tax.

The time needed to complete and file this form will vary depending on individual circumstances. The estimated average time is:

Recordkeeping . . . . . 6 hr., 13 min.

Learning about the law or the form . . . . . 2 hr., 59 min.

Preparing, copying, assembling, and sending the form to the IRS . . . . . 3 hr., 13 min.

If you have comments concerning the accuracy of these time estimates or suggestions for making this form more simple, we would be happy to hear from you. You can write to both the **Internal Revenue Service,** Attention: Reports Clearance Officer, T:FP, Washington, DC 20224; and the **Office of Management and Budget,** Paperwork Reduction Project (1545-0146), Washington, DC 20503. **DO NOT** send the tax form to either of these offices. Instead, see **Where To File** below.

General Instructions

Purpose.—To elect to be an "S corporation," a corporation must file Form 2553. The election permits the income of the S corporation to be taxed to the shareholders of the corporation rather than to the corporation itself, except as provided in Subchapter S of the Code. For more information, get Pub. 589, Tax Information on S Corporations.

Who May Elect.—A corporation may elect to be an S corporation only if it meets all of the following tests:

1. It is a domestic corporation.

2. It has no more than 35 shareholders. A husband and wife (and their estates) are treated as one shareholder for this requirement. All other persons are treated as separate shareholders.

3. It has only individuals, estates, or certain trusts as shareholders. See the instructions for Part III regarding qualified subchapter S trusts.

4. It has no nonresident alien shareholders.

5. It has only one class of stock (disregarding differences in voting rights). Generally, a corporation is treated as having only one class of stock if all outstanding shares of the corporation's stock confer identical rights to distribution and liquidation

proceeds. See Regulations section 1.1361-1(l) for more details.

6. It is not one of the following ineligible corporations:

a. A corporation that owns 80% or more of the stock of another corporation, unless the other corporation has not begun business and has no gross income;

b. A bank or thrift institution;

c. An insurance company subject to tax under the special rules of Subchapter L of the Code;

d. A corporation that has elected to be treated as a possessions corporation under section 936; or

e. A domestic international sales corporation (DISC) or former DISC.

7. It has a permitted tax year as required by section 1378 or makes a section 444 election to have a tax year other than a permitted tax year. Section 1378 defines a permitted tax year as a tax year ending December 31, or any other tax year for which the corporation establishes a business purpose to the satisfaction of the IRS. See Part II for details on requesting a fiscal tax year based on a business purpose or on making a section 444 election.

8. Each shareholder consents as explained in the instructions for Column K.

See sections 1361, 1362, and 1378 for additional information on the above tests.

Where To File.—File this election with the Internal Revenue Service Center listed below:

If the corporation's principal business, office, or agency is located in	Use the following Internal Revenue Service Center address
New Jersey, New York (New York City and counties of Nassau, Rockland, Suffolk, and Westchester)	Holtsville, NY 00501
New York (all other counties), Connecticut, Maine, Massachusetts, New Hampshire, Rhode Island, Vermont	Andover, MA 05501
Illinois, Iowa, Minnesota, Missouri, Wisconsin	Kansas City, MO 64999
Delaware, District of Columbia, Maryland, Pennsylvania, Virginia	Philadelphia, PA 19255
Florida, Georgia, South Carolina	Atlanta, GA 39901
Indiana, Kentucky, Michigan, Ohio, West Virginia	Cincinnati, OH 45999
Kansas, New Mexico, Oklahoma, Texas	Austin, TX 73301

Alaska, Arizona, California (counties of Alpine, Amador, Butte, Calaveras, Colusa, Contra Costa, Del Norte, El Dorado, Glenn, Humboldt, Lake, Lassen, Marin, Mendocino, Modoc, Napa, Nevada, Placer, Plumas, Sacramento, San Joaquin, Shasta, Sierra, Siskiyou, Solano, Sonoma, Sutter, Tehama, Trinity, Yolo, and Yuba), Colorado, Idaho, Montana, Nebraska, Nevada, North Dakota, Oregon, South Dakota, Utah, Washington, Wyoming	Ogden, UT 84201
California (all other counties), Hawaii	Fresno, CA 93888
Alabama, Arkansas, Louisiana, Mississippi, North Carolina, Tennessee	Memphis, TN 37501

When To Make the Election.—Complete and file Form 2553 (a) at any time before the 16th day of the third month of the tax year, if filed during the tax year the election is to take effect, or (b) at any time during the preceding tax year. An election made no later than 2 months and 15 days after the beginning of a tax year that is less than 2½ months long is treated as timely made for that tax year. An election made after the 15th day of the third month but before the end of the tax year is effective for the next year. For example, if a calendar tax year corporation makes the election in April 1994, it is effective for the corporation's 1995 calendar tax year. See section 1362(b) for more information.

Acceptance or Nonacceptance of Election.—The Service Center will notify the corporation if its election is accepted and when it will take effect. The corporation should generally receive a determination on its election within 60 days after it has filed Form 2553. If box Q1 in Part II is checked on page 2, the corporation will receive a ruling letter from the IRS in Washington, DC, that either approves or denies the selected tax year. When box Q1 is checked, it will generally take an additional 90 days for the Form 2553 to be accepted.

Do not file Form 1120S until the corporation is notified that its election has been accepted. If the corporation is now required to file Form 1120, U.S. Corporation Income Tax Return, or any other applicable tax return, continue filing it until the election takes effect.

Care should be exercised to ensure that the IRS receives the election. If the corporation is not notified of acceptance or nonacceptance of its election within 3 months

*Government forms may vary each year. Consult your current year's forms for complete information.

Form 2

IRS Form 2553: Election of Subchapter S Status with Instructions (continued)

of date of filing (date mailed), or within 6 months if box Q1 is checked, please take follow-up action by corresponding with the Service Center where the corporation filed the election. If the IRS questions whether Form 2553 was filed, an acceptable proof of filing is: (a) certified or registered mail receipt (timely filed); (b) Form 2553 with accepted stamp; (c) Form 2553 with stamped IRS received date; or (d) IRS letter stating that Form 2553 has been accepted.

End of Election.— Once the election is made, it stays in effect for all years until it is terminated. During the 5 years after the election is terminated under section 1362(d), the corporation (or a successor corporation) can make another election on Form 2553 only with IRS consent. See Regulations section 1.1362-5 for more details.

Specific Instructions
Part I

Part I must be completed by all corporations.

Name and Address of Corporation.—Enter the true corporate name as set forth in the corporate charter or other legal document creating it. If the corporation's mailing address is the same as someone else's, such as a shareholder's, please enter "c/o" and this person's name following the name of the corporation. Include the suite, room, or other unit number after the street address. If the Post Office does not deliver to the street address and the corporation has a P.O. box, show the box number instead of the street address. If the corporation changed its name or address after applying for its EIN, be sure to check the box in item G of Part I.

Item A. Employer Identification Number.—If the corporation has applied for an employer identification number (EIN) but has not received it, enter "applied for." If the corporation does not have an EIN, it should apply for one on **Form SS-4,** Application for Employer Identification Number, available from most IRS and Social Security Administration offices.

Item D. Effective Date of Election.—Enter the beginning effective date (month, day, year) of the tax year requested for the S corporation. Generally, this will be the beginning date of the tax year for which the ending effective date is required to be shown in item I, Part I. For a new corporation (first year the corporation exists) it will generally be the date required to be shown in item H, Part I. The tax year of a new corporation starts on the date that it has shareholders, acquires assets, or begins doing business, whichever happens first. If the effective date for item D for a newly formed corporation is later than the date in item H, the corporation should file Form 1120 or Form 1120-A, for the tax period between these dates.

Column K. Shareholders' Consent Statement.—Each shareholder who owns (or is deemed to own) stock at the time the election is made must consent to the election. If the election is made during the corporation's tax year for which it first takes effect, any person who held stock at any time during the part of that year that occurs before the election is made, must consent to the election, even though the person may have sold or transferred his or her stock before the

election is made. Each shareholder consents by signing and dating in column K or signing and dating a separate consent statement described below.

An election made during the first 2½ months of the tax year is effective for the following tax year if any person who held stock in the corporation during the part of the tax year before the election was made, and who did not hold stock at the time the election was made, did not consent to the election.

If a husband and wife have a community interest in the stock or in the income from it, both must consent. Each tenant in common, joint tenant, and tenant by the entirety also must consent.

A minor's consent is made by the minor or the legal representative of the minor, or by a natural or adoptive parent of the minor if no legal representative has been appointed.

The consent of an estate is made by an executor or administrator.

If stock is owned by a trust that is a qualified shareholder, the deemed owner of the trust must consent. See section 1361(c)(2) for details regarding qualified trusts that may be shareholders and rules on determining who is the deemed owner of the trust.

Continuation sheet or separate consent statement.—If you need a continuation sheet or use a separate consent statement, attach it to Form 2553. The separate consent statement must contain the name, address, and employer identification number of the corporation and the shareholder information requested in columns J through N of Part I. If you want, you may combine all the shareholders' consents in one statement.

Column L.—Enter the number of shares of stock each shareholder owns and the dates the stock was acquired. If the election is made during the corporation's tax year for which it first takes effect, do not list the shares of stock for those shareholders who sold or transferred all of their stock before the election was made. However, these shareholders must still consent to the election for it to be effective for the tax year.

Column M.—Enter the social security number of each shareholder who is an individual. Enter the employer identification number of each shareholder that is an estate or a qualified trust.

Column N.—Enter the month and day that each shareholder's tax year ends. If a shareholder is changing his or her tax year, enter the tax year the shareholder is changing to, and attach an explanation indicating the present tax year and the basis for the change (e.g., automatic revenue procedure or letter ruling request).

If the election is made during the corporation's tax year for which it first takes effect, you do not have to enter the tax year of any shareholder who sold or transferred all of his or her stock before the election was made.

Signature.—Form 2553 must be signed by the president, treasurer, assistant treasurer, chief accounting officer, or other corporate officer (such as tax officer) authorized to sign.

Part II

Complete Part II if you selected a tax year ending on any date other than December 31

(other than a 52-53-week tax year ending with reference to the month of December).

Box P1.—Attach a statement showing separately for each month the amount of gross receipts for the most recent 47 months as required by section 4.03(3) of Revenue Procedure 87-32, 1987-2 C.B. 396. A corporation that does not have a 47-month period of gross receipts cannot establish a natural business year under section 4.01(1).

Box Q1.—For examples of an acceptable business purpose for requesting a fiscal tax year, see Revenue Ruling 87-57, 1987-2 C.B. 117.

In addition to a statement showing the business purpose for the requested fiscal year, you must attach the other information necessary to meet the ruling request requirements of Revenue Procedure 93-1, 1993-1 I.R.B. 10 (updated annually). Also attach a statement that shows separately the amount of gross receipts from sales or services (and inventory costs, if applicable) for each of the 36 months preceding the effective date of the election to be an S corporation. If the corporation has been in existence for fewer than 36 months, submit figures for the period of existence.

If you check box Q1, you must also pay a user fee of $200 (subject to change). Do not pay the fee when filing Form 2553. The Service Center will send Form 2553 to the IRS in Washington, DC, who, in turn, will notify the corporation that the fee is due. See Revenue Procedure 93-23, 1993-19 I.R.B. 6.

Box Q2.—If the corporation makes a back-up section 444 election for which it is qualified, then the election must be exercised in the event the business purpose request is not approved. Under certain circumstances, the tax year requested under the back-up section 444 election may be different than the tax year requested under business purpose. See **Form 8716,** Election To Have a Tax Year Other Than a Required Tax Year, for details on making a back-up section 444 election.

Boxes Q2 and R2.—If the corporation is not qualified to make the section 444 election after making the item Q2 back-up section 444 election or indicating its intention to make the election in item R1, and therefore it later files a calendar year return, it should write "Section 444 Election Not Made" in the top left corner of the 1st calendar year Form 1120S it files.

Part III

Certain Qualified Subchapter S Trusts (QSSTs) may make the QSST election required by section 1361(d)(2) in Part III. Part III may be used to make the QSST election only if corporate stock has been transferred to the trust on or before the date on which the corporation makes its election to be an S corporation. However, a statement can be used in lieu of Part III to make the election.

Note: *Part III may be used only in conjunction with making the Part I election (i.e., Form 2553 cannot be filed with only Part III completed).*

The deemed owner of the QSST must also consent to the S corporation election in column K, page 1, of Form 2553. See section 1361(c)(2).

Page 2

*Government forms may vary each year. Consult your current year's forms for complete information.

Form 3

Articles of Organization of Limited Liability Company

STATE OF CALIFORNIA
ACTING SECRETARY OF STATE
TONY MILLER

LIMITED LIABILITY COMPANY
ARTICLES OF ORGANIZATION

IMPORTANT - Read instructions before completing the form.
This document is presented for filing pursuant to Section 17050 of the California Corporations Code.

1. Limited liability company name:

   (End the name with "LLC" or "Limited Liability Company". No periods between the letters in "LLC". "Limited" and "Company" may be abbreviated to "Ltd." and "Co.")

2. Latest date on which the limited liability company is to dissolve:

3. The purpose of the limited liability company is to engage in any lawful act or activity for which a limited liability company may be organized under the Beverly-Killea Limited Liability Company Act.

4. Enter the name of initial agent for service of process and check the appropriate provision below:

   _____ , which is

   [   ]   an individual residing in California. Proceed to Item 5.

   [   ]   a corporation which has filed a certificate pursuant to Section 1505 of the California Corporations Code. Skip Item 5 and proceed to Item 6.

5. If the initial agent for service of process is an individual, enter a business or residential street address in California:

   Street address:

   City: State: CALIFORNIA   Zip Code:

6. The limited liability company will be managed by : (check one)

   [   ] one manager   [   ] more than one manager   [   ] limited liability company members

7. If other matters are to be included in the articles of organization attach one or more separate pages.

   Number of pages attached, if any:

8. It is hereby declared that I am the person who executed this instrument, which execution is my act and deed.

   For Secretary of State Use

   _____
   Signature of organizer

   _____
   Type or print name of organizer

   Date: _____ , 19 ___

---

*Government forms may vary each year. Consult your current year's forms for complete information.

Form 4

UCC-1: Standard Financing Statement

Appendix

```
                              STATE OF CALIFORNIA
         UNIFORM COMMERCIAL CODE — FINANCING STATEMENT — FORM UCC-1        (price class 13C)
WOLCOTTS FORM UCC-1CA          IMPORTANT — Read instructions on back before filling out form

         This FINANCING STATEMENT is presented for filing and will remain effective, with certain exceptions,
           for five years from the date of filing, pursuant to Section 9403 of the California Uniform Commercial Code.
```

1. DEBTOR (LAST NAME FIRST—IF AN INDIVIDUAL)	1A. SOCIAL SECURITY OR FEDERAL TAX NO.	
1B. MAILING ADDRESS	1C. CITY, STATE	1D. ZIP CODE
2. ADDITIONAL DEBTOR (IF ANY) (LAST NAME FIRST—IF AN INDIVIDUAL)	2A. SOCIAL SECURITY OR FEDERAL TAX NO.	
2B. MAILING ADDRESS	2C. CITY, STATE	2D. ZIP CODE
3. DEBTOR'S TRADE NAMES OR STYLES (IF ANY)	3A. FEDERAL TAX NUMBER	

```
4. SECURED PARTY                                          4A. SOCIAL SECURITY NO . FEDERAL TAX NO
   NAME                                                       OR BANK TRANSIT AND A B A. NO.
   MAILING ADDRESS
   CITY                    STATE              ZIP CODE
5. ASSIGNEE OF SECURED PARTY  (IF ANY)                    5A. SOCIAL SECURITY NO., FEDERAL TAX NO
   NAME                                                       OR BANK TRANSIT AND A B A. NO.
   MAILING ADDRESS
   CITY                    STATE              ZIP CODE
```

6. This FINANCING STATEMENT covers the following types or items of property **(include description of real property on which located and owner of record when required by instruction 4).**

```
7. CHECK    [X]   7A. [ ] PRODUCTS OF COLLATERAL     7B. DEBTOR(S) SIGNATURE NOT REQUIRED IN ACCORDANCE WITH
   IF APPLICABLE           ARE ALSO COVERED               INSTRUCTION 5(#) ITEM:
                                                          [ ](1)  [ ](2)  [ ](3)  [ ](4)

8. CHECK    [X]        [ ] DEBTOR IS A "TRANSMITTING UTILITY" IN ACCORDANCE WITH UCC § 9105 (1) (n)
   IF APPLICABLE
```

9. DATE:	C O D E	10. THIS SPACE FOR USE OF FILING OFFICER (DATE, TIME, FILE NUMBER AND FILING OFFICER)
► SIGNATURE(S) OF DEBTOR(S)	1	
TYPE OR PRINT NAME(S) OF DEBTOR(S)	2	
► SIGNATURE(S) OF SECURED PARTY(IES)	3	
	4	
TYPE OR PRINT NAME(S) OF SECURED PARTY(IES)	5	
	6	
11. Return copy to:	7	
NAME	8	
ADDRESS	9	
CITY	0	
STATE		
ZIP CODE		
(1) FILING OFFICER COPY FORM UCC-1 Approved by the Secretary of State		

*Government forms may vary each year. Consult your current year's forms for complete information.

Form 4

UCC-1: Standard Financing Statement (continued)

INSTRUCTIONS

1. PLEASE TYPE THIS FORM USING BLACK TYPEWRITER RIBBON.

2. If the space provided for any item is inadequate:
   a. Note "Cont'd." in the appropriate space(s).
   b. Continue the item(s) preceded by the Item No. on an additional 8½"x11" sheet.
   c. Head each additional sheet with the Debtor's name (last name first for individuals) appearing in Item No. 1 of this form. Be sure to attach a copy of the additional sheet to each copy of the form.

3. NUMERICAL IDENTIFICATION:
   a. If the Debtor, Secured Party or Assignee is an individual, include Social Security number in the appropriate space. Disclosure of Social Security number is optional for the filing of this statement. It will be used to assist in correctly identifying individuals with similar names. (UCC § 9403[5])
   b. If the Debtor, Secured Party or Assignee is other than an individual or a bank, show Federal Taxpayer Number in the appropriate space.
   c. If the Secured Party or Assignee is a bank, show Transit and ABA number in the appropriate space. This must be the complete 10 digit number.

4. COLLATERAL DESCRIPTION—Item 6
   a. If the financing statement covers crops growing or to be grown, the statement must also contain a description of the real estate concerned in accordance with UCC § 9402(1).
   b. If the financing statement covers timber to be cut or covers minerals or the like, oil or gas or accounts subject to UCC § 9103(5), the statement must show that it covers this type of collateral and the statement must also show it is to be recorded in the real estate records, and the financing statement must contain a description of the real estate sufficient if it were contained in a mortgage of the real estate to give constructive notice of the mortgage under the law of this State. If the debtor does not have an interest of record in the real estate, the financing statement must show the name of a record owner in Item No. 6.

5. SIGNATURES:
   Before mailing, be sure that the financing statement has been properly signed. A financing statement requires the signature of the debtor only *except* under the following circumstances. If any of these circumstances apply, check the appropriate box in item 7B and enter required information in Item 6.
   a. Under the provisions of UCC § 9402(2) a financing statement is sufficient when it is signed by the secured party alone if it is filed to perfect a security interest in:

   (1) collateral already subject to a security interest in another jurisdiction when it is brought into this State or when the debtor's location is changed to this State. Such a financing statement must state that the collateral was brought into this State or that the debtor's location was changed to this State.

   (2) proceeds under UCC § 9306, if the security interest in the original collateral was perfected. Such a financing statement must describe the original collateral and give the date of filing and the file number of the prior financing statement.

   (3) collateral as to which the filing has lapsed. Such a financing statement must include a statement to the effect that the prior financing statement has lapsed and give the date of filing and the file number of the prior financing statement.

   (4) collateral acquired after a change of name, identity or corporate structure of the debtor. Such a financing statement must include a statement that the name, identity or corporate structure of the debtor has been changed and give the date of filing and the file number of the prior financing statement and the name of the debtor as shown in the prior financing statement.

6. FILING FEE—PROPER PLACE TO FILE:
   Enclose filing fee of .   payable to the appropriate Filing Officer. Financing statements and related papers pertaining to consumer goods should be filed with the County Recorder in the county of the debtor's residence, or if the debtor is not a resident of this State, then in the office of the County Recorder of the county in which the goods are kept. When the collateral is crops growing or to be grown, timber to be cut, or minerals or the like (including oil and gas), or accounts subject to UCC § 9103(5), then filing is with the County Recorder where the property is located. In all other cases, filing is with the Secretary of State.

7. REMOVE SECURED PARTY AND DEBTOR COPIES.
   Send the *original and first copy* with interleaved carbon paper to the Filing Officer with the correct filing fee. The original will be retained by the Filing Officer. The copy will be returned with the filing date and time stamped thereon. *Indicate the name and mailing address of the person or firm to whom the copy is to be returned in Item No. 11.*

   * For current fee to the Secretary of State Call (916) 445-8061

---

*Government forms may vary each year. Consult your current year's forms for complete information.

Form 5

UCC-3: Request for Information or Copies

REQUEST FOR INFORMATION OR COPIES. Present in Duplicate to Filing Officer

1. ☐ INFORMATION REQUEST. Filing officer please furnish certificate showing whether there is on file any presently effective financing statement naming the Debtor listed below and any statement of assignment thereof, and if there is, giving the date and hour of filing of each such statement and the names and addresses of each secured party named therein.

1A. DEBTOR (LAST NAME FIRST)		1B. SOC. SEC. OR FED. TAX NO.

1C. MAILING ADDRESS	1D. CITY, STATE	1E. ZIP CODE

1F. Date _____ 19___ Signature of Requesting Party _____

2. CERTIFICATE:

FILE NUMBER	DATE AND HOUR OF FILING	NAME(S) AND ADDRESS(ES) OF SECURED PARTY(IES) AND ASSIGNEE(S), IF ANY

The undersigned filing officer hereby certifies that the above listing is a record of all presently effective financing statements and statements of assignment which name the above debtor and which are on file in my office as of _____19_____ at_____ ___M.

_____19_____
(DATE)

_____ (FILING OFFICER)

By:_____

3. ☐ COPY REQUEST. Filing officer please furnish _____ copy(ies) of each page of the following statements concerning the debtors listed below ☐ Financing Statement ☐ Amendments ☐ Statements of Assignment ☐ Continuation Statements ☐ Statement of Release ☐ Termination Statement ☐ All Statements on file.

FILE NUMBER	DATE OF FILING	NAME(S) AND MAILING ADDRESS(ES) OF DEBTOR(S)	DEBTORS SOC. SEC. OR FED. TAX NO.

Date_____ 19___ Signature of Requesting Party _____

4. CERTIFICATE:

The undersigned filing officer hereby certifies that the attached copies are true and exact copies of all statements requested above.

_____ 19___
(DATE)

_____ (FILING OFFICER)

By_____

5. *Mail Information or Copies To*

NAME
MAILING ADDRESS
CITY AND STATE

*Government forms may vary each year. Consult your current year's forms for complete information.

Form 5

UCC-3: Request for Information or Copies (continued)

PROCEDURES FOR FILING UCC-3'S

INFORMATION REQUEST ONLY: Check box #1 and complete all items.
(1A thru 1F; item 1B is optional.)
May contain only one debtor name and
address. If more than one address
is required for a specific debtor,
show "ANY ADDRESS" in item 1C.

Fee: $11.00

COPIES ONLY REQUEST: Check box #3 and indicate desired
documents by checking appropriate box.
List file number(s), debtor name(s)
and address(s) or "Any Address". Requesting party MUST sign for copies.
If signature, debtor name or file number
is not shown, UCC-3 will be rejected.

Fee: $1.00 per document and .50¢ per
attachment.

Requestor MUST complete Mail Information portion of form; a request cannot be processed without this information. UCC-3's must
contain a carbon copy for each request which will be returned to
the address in section 5.

Effective January 1, 1986, Copies Only Requests submitted to the
Uniform Commercial Code Division of the Secretary of State's Office
must include the file number(s) and the debtor(s) name for which
you are requesting copies. Requests that do not include the file
number(s) and debtor name(s) will be rejected.

If you do not know the file number you can submit an Information
Request and check for $11.00 to the UCC Division and receive a cer-
tificate showing the file number(s), or you can check both the
Information and the Copy Request boxes and submit along with a
check that reads: "Not to Exceed $35.00", exact amount to be com-
pleted by Sec. of State.

Mail requests to: Secretary of State
UCC Division
P.O. Box 1738
Sacramento, CA 95808

Rev. 1/98

*Government forms may vary each year. Consult your current year's forms for complete information.

Form 6

Agreement for Sale of Assets
of
[Corporation]

This Agreement is made this [date], between [Corporation] having its principal office located at [location] (referred to as "Seller"), and, [Buyer] having its principal office located at [location] (referred to as "Buyer").

RECITALS

Seller owns and operates [describe business], and desires to sell to Buyer the purchased assets, as hereinafter defined, subject to the assumed liabilities, as hereinafter defined, on the terms and conditions herein set forth.

Buyer desires to purchase the same assets, and is willing to assume all obligations and liabilities of Seller of these assets as hereinafter defined, on the terms and conditions herein set forth.

In consideration of the mutual covenants, agreements, representations, and warranties contained in this Agreement, the parties hereto agree as follows:

ASSETS BEING SOLD AND PURCHASED

Upon the terms and subject to the conditions of this Agreement, at the Closing, Seller shall sell, transfer, and deliver, or cause to be sold, transferred and delivered, to Buyer and Buyer shall purchase from Seller, all of Seller's right, title and interest in and to the following assets: [list assets]. It is expressly agreed that Seller is not selling, assigning, conveying, or transferring to Buyer any assets, interests, rights, and properties of Seller, other than those specifically conveyed to Buyer pursuant to this section.

PURCHASE PRICE

On the terms and subject to the conditions herein expressed, in consideration of and in exchange for the purchased assets, Buyer shall pay a purchase price according to the following schedule: [list purchase price and terms of payment]. The purchase price shall be allocated among the assets in the following manner: [list allocation of purchase price for the assets sold].

ASSUMPTION OF LIABILITIES

On the terms and subject to the conditions herein expressed, in consideration of and in exchange for the purchased assets, Buyer shall pay the purchase price pursuant to this Agreement and assume the following debts, obligations, and liabilities, (hereinafter collectively referred to as "Assumed liabilities"): (a.) All liabilities and obligations which relate to the assets being sold and purchased in accordance with Section I of this Agreement; and (b.) All liabilities and obligations arising from and after the Closing date under the contracts pursuant to the terms thereof; and (c.) All liabilities and obligations specifically undertaken by Buyer pursuant to other provisions of this Agreement. Buyer shall not be liable for any obligations or liabilities of Seller of any kind and nature other than those specifically assumed under this section. Buyer will indemnify Seller against any and all liability under the contracts and obligations assumed hereunder, provided that Seller is not in default under any of the contracts or obligations at the date of Closing.

CLOSING/INSTRUMENTS OF TRANSFER

The completion of the transactions contemplated by this Agreement (hereinafter referred to as the "Closing") shall take place on the Closing date at [time]. The Closing shall take place at [location]. The Closing date shall be [date], provided that the conditions precedent and contingencies set forth in accordance with this Agreement are satisfied. At the Closing:

(a.) Seller shall deliver to Buyer all such bills of sale, contract assignments, consents or other documents and instruments of sale, assignment, conveyance, and transfer as are appropriate or necessary with the terms of this Agreement and such other documents as Buyer may reasonably request to carry out the purposes of this Agreement; and,

(b.) Buyer shall deliver to Seller the Closing payments in accordance with this Agreement; documents evidencing assumptions by Buyer of the Assumed liabilities and such other documents as Seller may reasonably request to carry out the purposes of this Agreement.

ASSIGNMENT OF LEASE AND CONTRACT RIGHTS

If any lease or contract assignable to Buyer under this Agreement may not be assigned without the consent of the other party thereto, Seller shall use its best efforts to obtain the consent of the other party to such assignment.

JOINT COVENANTS, REPRESENTATIONS AND WARRANTIES

Buyer and Seller shall cooperate and use their best efforts to prepare all instruments of transfer or other documents as promptly as practicable; and

Buyer and Seller shall act in good faith and fair dealing in facilitating, maintaining, and carrying out the duties and obligations of this Agreement.

SELLER'S COVENANTS, REPRESENTATIONS AND WARRANTIES

Seller represents and warrants as follows: (a.) <u>Organization</u>. Seller is a [Sole Proprietorship, Partnership, or Corporation] organized, existing, and in good standing under the laws of the State of [list state of Incorporation]; (b.) <u>Authority</u>. Seller has approved the sale and purchase of assets, as described by this Agreement and has authorized or ratified the execution, delivery and performance of this Agreement by Seller; (c.) <u>Financial Statements</u>. Seller has delivered to Buyer copies of its financial statements, as requested by Buyer; (d.) <u>Title to Assets</u>. Seller is the owner of and has good and marketable title to all assets, which are to be sold and purchased in accordance with the terms of this Agreement, free of all restrictions on transfer or assignment and of all encumbrances except: (1.) as otherwise disclosed in the financial statements or in this Agreement; (2.) the liens for taxes not yet due and payable; (e.) <u>Absence of Default.</u> Seller is not in default in payment of any of its obligations under any agreement or contract for the assets listed in this Agreement; (f.) <u>Absence of Pending or Threatened Litigation.</u> To the best of Seller's knowledge, no proceedings, judgments, or liens are now pending or threatened against the assets listed in section I of this Agreement; (g.) <u>Seller's Expenses and Liabilities.</u> Seller shall pay any applicable tax, other than sales tax, arising out of the transfer of assets. Seller shall be responsible for any expense or tax, other than sales tax, of any kind related to any period before the date of execution of this Agreement.

BUYER'S REPRESENTATIONS AND WARRANTIES

Buyer represents and warrants as follows: (a.) <u>Organization.</u> Buyer is a [Sole Proprietorship, Partnership, or Corporation] and has all requisite power and authority to enter into and perform and carry out this Agreement and the transaction contemplated hereby; (b.)

<u>Authority</u>. Buyer is authorized to acquire articles of Incorporation authorize it to acquire and operate the properties now owned and operated by Seller, which are being sold and purchased in accordance with this Agreement. Buyer has taken all requisite action to authorize the execution and delivery of this Agreement by Buyer and the performance and consummation of the transactions contemplated hereby, and this Agreement has been duly executed and delivered by Buyer and is binding upon and enforceable against Buyer in accordance with its terms; (c.) <u>Books and Records.</u> Buyer shall afford Seller, or Seller's representative, access to inspect during regular business hours upon five business days prior written demand, Buyer's records and books of Seller's list of customer accounts on a monthly basis, provided that Seller's investigation and use of same shall be for the sole purpose to ensure payment of Buyer's liabilities to Seller; (d.) <u>Financial Statements.</u> Buyer shall deliver to Seller copies of financial statements of Buyer on a quarterly basis throughout the pay out period, all of which have been prepared in accordance with generally accepted accounting principles applied on a consistent basis, including, with respect to each of the Buyer's last fiscal years, a balance sheet and a statement of profit and loss accounts and surplus and quarterly financial statements for the sole purpose to ensure payment of Buyer's liabilities to Seller; (f.) <u>Note.</u> At the date of Closing, Buyer agrees to execute a Note to secure payments as reflected in this Agreement.

CONTINGENCIES OR CONDITIONS TO BUYER'S OBLIGATIONS

The obligations of Buyer under this Agreement are subject to fulfillment of the following contingencies or conditions: (a.) The instruments and conveyances of transfer executed and delivered by Seller in accordance with this Agreement shall, to the best of Seller's knowledge, be valid in accordance with their terms and shall effectively vest in Buyer good and marketable title to the assets as contemplated by this Agreement, contingent upon the liabilities and obligations assumed by Buyer as provided in this Agreement; (b.) All assets and equipment being sold and purchased as listed in this Agreement are in good and operable condition and working order to the best of Seller's knowledge as of the date of Closing; (c.) Representations and warranties made by Seller in this Agreement shall be true and accurate in all material respects on the date of Closing; (d.) All corporate and shareholder proceedings required to be

Form 6

taken by Seller to authorize it to enter into this Agreement have been properly taken [if Seller is a Corporation].

CONTINGENCIES OR CONDITIONS TO SELLER'S OBLIGATIONS

All obligations of Seller under this Agreement are subject to fulfillment of the following contingencies or conditions: (a.) Representations and warranties made by Buyer in this Agreement shall be true and accurate in all material respects on the date of Closing; (b.) Buyer shall have performed and complied in all material respects with all agreements and covenants on its part required to be performed or complied with on or prior to the Closing date; (c.) All corporate and shareholder proceedings required to be taken by Buyer to authorize it to enter into this Agreement have been properly taken [if Buyer is a Corporation].

INSURANCE

Buyer shall maintain sufficient insurance on all tangible assets listed in this Agreement and Buyer shall pay all costs associated with such insurance. Buyer agrees to keep the assets in good order and repair and free of all taxes, liens and encumbrances, other than those existing at the date of Closing.

INDEMNIFICATION

(a). Indemnification of Seller. Buyer shall indemnify and hold Seller harmless against any and all claims, demands, losses, costs, obligations, and liabilities that Seller may incur or suffer as a result of Buyer's: (i) breach of this agreement, and (ii) any inaccuracy or misrepresentation in or breach of any covenant, warranty, representation or agreement made by Buyer in this Agreement; (b). Indemnification of Buyer. Seller shall indemnify and hold Buyer harmless against any and all claims, demands, losses, costs, obligations, and liabilities that Buyer may incur or suffer as a result of Seller's: (i) breach of this agreement, and (ii) any inaccuracy or misrepresentation in or breach of any covenant, warranty, representation or agreement made by Seller in this Agreement.

EXHIBITS INCORPORATED BY REFERENCE

All exhibits referred to herein are incorporated by reference and are so incorporated for all purposes.

TIME OF ESSENCE

Time is of the essence in this Agreement.

COUNTERPARTS

The Agreement may be executed simultaneously in two or more counterparts, each of which shall be deemed an original, however all of which shall constitute but one and the same instrument.

BINDING EFFECT ON REPRESENTATIVES AND SUCCESSORS

This Agreement shall be binding upon and inure to the benefit or the representatives, heirs, estates, successors and assign of the parties to this Agreement. Nothing expressed or implied in this Agreement is intended, or shall be construed, to confer upon or give any person, firm, or Corporation, other than the parties, their successors and assigns, any benefits, rights or remedies under or by reason of this Agreement, except to the extent of any contrary provision of this Agreement.

ASSIGNMENT OF THIS AGREEMENT

Buyer's interest in this Agreement shall not be sold, assigned, pledged, encumbered, or transferred by Buyer without the written consent of Seller. In the event of an assignment of Buyer's interest by operation of law or in the event there shall be filed by or against Buyer in any court pursuant to any statute either of the United States or any state, a petition in bankruptcy, or insolvency or for reorganization, or for the appointment of a receiver or trustee of all or a portions of Buyer's property, or if Buyer makes an assignment for the benefit of creditors, or petitions for or enters into an arrangement, then in any such event, Seller may, at its option terminate this Agreement and shall have all remedies available.

SEVERABILITY

Should any provision of this Agreement presently or hereafter in effect be deemed or held to be invalid, such invalidity shall not adversely affect the other provisions herein contained unless such invalidity shall make impossible the function of this Agreement; in such case the parties shall promptly adopt new provisions to take the place of the invalid provisions.

WAVIER

The failure of any party to insist upon the prompt and punctual performance of any term or condition in this Agreement, or the failure of any party to exercise any right or remedy under the terms of this

Agreement on any one or more occasions shall not constitute a waiver of that or any other term, condition, right or remedy on that or any subsequent occasion.

MODIFICATION

Any modification of this Agreement must be in writing and signed by the parties to this Agreement.

EXPENSES

Seller and Buyer shall each pay all costs and expenses incurred or to be incurred by each of them respectively in negotiating and preparing this Agreement and in carrying out the transactions contemplated thereby.

ATTORNEYS' FEES

If either party to this Agreement shall employ legal counsel to protect its rights under this Agreement or to enforce any term or provision of this Agreement, then the party prevailing in any such legal action shall have the right to recover from the other party all of its reasonable attorneys' fees, costs, and expenses incurred in relation to such claim.

NOTICES

All notices to be given shall be given in writing and shall be delivered personally or by registered or certified mail, postage prepaid, as follows: If to buyer, to the first listed address for Buyer located in this Agreement. If to seller, to the first listed address for Seller located in this Agreement.

LAW GOVERNING

This Agreement shall be governed by and construed under the laws of the State of [list state].

ENTIRE AGREEMENT

This Agreement, including the exhibits referred to herein, contains the entire Agreement between the parties with respect to the transaction contemplated herein.

The parties have executed this Agreement in the City of _____, County of _____ , State of _____, on the date first above written.

"Seller"   "Buyer"

_____   _____

By: By:

Form 7

Agreement for Purchase and Sale of Common Stock

This agreement is made and entered into by and between [Name of Seller], sometimes hereinafter referred to as "Seller," and [name of Buyers], sometimes hereinafter referred to as "Buyers,"

WHEREAS, Seller is the owner of [number] shares of common stock ("stock") of [name of Corporation], a [state of Incorporation] Corporation, hereinafter sometimes referred to as "Company"; and

WHEREAS, Seller is willing to sell, and Buyers are willing to purchase said Seller's stock in Company upon the terms and conditions hereinafter set forth.

NOW, THEREFORE, IT IS AGREED as follows:

PURCHASE OF COMMON STOCK

Seller agrees to sell, and Buyers agree to buy Seller's stock in Company for the sum of [amount of sale]. The purchase price shall be paid as follows: Cash to the Seller at the closing of [amount]; and by the execution and delivery to Seller of a promissory note in the amount of [amount of note], bearing interest at [X] percent (X%) per annum, [date of first payment due] with principal and interest payable in monthly installments, beginning [date of first payment date] and continuing on the first day each month until paid in full.

ASSIGNMENT AND TRANSFER.

Seller hereby sells and transfers to Buyers his [number] shares (and any other shares) of common stock in Company. Seller shall execute and deliver to Buyers at the closing, or at any subsequent time as may be demanded by Buyers, such bill of sale, assignment or other documents evidencing the conveyance of Seller's common stock of the Company to Buyers. At the closing, Seller shall deliver such certificate or certificates evidencing such shares, duly endorsed in blank, to Buyers, naming [name of agent], as his agent for transferring said shares on the books and records of the Corporation as herein provided.

WARRANTIES OF SELLER

Seller hereby represents and warrants that he is the owner, beneficially and of record, of said [number] shares of common stock of

Company free and clear of all liens, encumbrances, security agreements, equities, options, claims, charges and restrictions. Seller further represents that these are the only shares or other interest in the Company which he owns. Seller has full power to transfer the common stock without obtaining the consent or approval of any person or entity.

LIABILITIES

Seller warrants and represents that he has not knowingly insured any liabilities in the name of the Corporation which are obligations of the Corporation. Seller agrees to indemnify and hold Buyers free and harmless from any liabilities knowingly incurred by Seller in the name of the Corporation which are not reflected on the books and records of the company on the date of this agreement.

RECOVERY OF COSTS

If any legal action is brought for the enforcement of this Agreement or because of an alleged dispute, breach, default or misrepresentation in connection with any of the provisions of this Agreement, the successful or prevailing party shall be entitled to recover reasonable attorney's fees and other costs incurred in that action or proceeding in addition to any other relief to which said party may be entitled.

SURVIVAL OF REPRESENTATIONS

Except as herein specifically provided, the representations and warranties made by any party hereto, and the obligations of any party to be performed hereunder, shall survive and continue beyond the transfer date of said Company interest.

CLOSING DATE

This transaction shall close on [date] at [time], at [location], or any other day prior thereto when all documents herein described have been delivered.

COSTS OF CLOSING

Each party shall be solely responsible for its own attorney's fees and costs in connection with the drafting and negotiation of this agreement.

IN WITNESS WHEREOF, the parties have executed this Agreement for Purchase and Sale of Common Stock this _____ day of _____, 19_____.

_____   _____

          "Seller"   _____
"Buyer"

The undersigned, [name of spouse], spouse of [name of seller] (seller), hereby consents to the terms of this agreement.

_____

          "Spouse of Seller"

Form 8

Fictitious Business Name Statement

LOS ANGELES COUNTY CLERK BUSINESS FILING AND REGISTRATION 111 NORTH HILL STREET, ROOM 106 LOS ANGELES, CA 90012	**REMINDER** 1. Submit Original and 3 copies. 2. Filing Fee $10.00. 3. Add $2.00 per additional name. 4. Provide self-addressed stamped envelope. 5. Make check payable to: LOS ANGELES COUNTY CLERK	

FICTITIOUS BUSINESS NAME STATEMENT

1. ☐ FIRST FILING OR ☐ RENEWAL FILING AND CURRENT REGISTRATION NO. _____

THE FOLLOWING PERSON(S) IS (ARE) DOING BUSINESS AS: SEE REVERSE SIDE FOR INSTRUCTIONS

2. FICTITIOUS BUSINESS NAME(S)
a.   b.
                                     c.

3. STREET ADDRESS, CITY AND STATE OF PRINCIPAL PLACE OF BUSINESS IN CALIFORNIA   (P.O. BOX ALONE NOT ACCEPTABLE)   ZIP CODE

4. FULL NAME OF REGISTRANT (IF CORPORATION—SHOW STATE OF INCORPORATION)

NOTE: PRINCIPAL PLACE OF BUSINESS MUST BE LOCATED IN L.A. COUNTY

RESIDENCE STREET ADDRESS	CITY	STATE	ZIP CODE

FULL NAME OF REGISTRANT (IF CORPORATION—SHOW STATE OF INCORPORATION)

RESIDENCE STREET ADDRESS	CITY	STATE	ZIP CODE

FULL NAME OF REGISTRANT (IF CORPORATION—SHOW STATE OF INCORPORATION)

RESIDENCE STREET ADDRESS	CITY	STATE	ZIP CODE

FULL NAME OF REGISTRANT (IF CORPORATION—SHOW STATE OF INCORPORATION)

RESIDENCE STREET ADDRESS	CITY	STATE	ZIP CODE

5. THIS BUSINESS IS CONDUCTED BY ☐ AN INDIVIDUAL ☐ A GENERAL PARTNERSHIP ☐ A LIMITED PARTNERSHIP ☐ AN UNINCORPORATED ASSOCIATION OTHER THAN A PARTNERSHIP ☐ A CORPORATION ☐ A BUSINESS TRUST ☐ CO-PARTNERS ☐ HUSBAND AND WIFE ☐ JOINT VENTURE ☐ OTHER _____ **(CHECK ONE ONLY)**

6. THE REGISTRANT COMMENCED TO TRANSACT BUSINESS UNDER THE FICTITIOUS NAME OR NAMES LISTED ABOVE ON (DATE): _____

7. IF REGISTRANT IS NOT A CORPORATION SIGN BELOW:
SIGNED (1) _____
SIGNED (2) _____
TYPED OR PRINTED (1) _____
TYPED OR PRINTED (2) _____

8. IF REGISTRANT A CORPORATION SIGN BELOW:
CORPORATION NAME _____
SIGNATURE _____
TITLE _____
ATTACH A COPY OF ARTICLES OF INCORPORATION

THIS STATEMENT WAS FILED WITH THE COUNTY CLERK OF LOS ANGELES COUNTY ON DATE INDICATED BY FILE STAMP ABOVE

NOTICE—THIS FICTITIOUS NAME STATEMENT EXPIRES 5 YRS FROM THE DATE IT WAS FILED AS SHOWN ABOVE. A NEW FICTITIOUS BUSINESS NAME STATEMENT MUST BE FILED PRIOR TO THAT DATE.

THE FILING OF THIS STATEMENT DOES NOT OF ITSELF AUTHORIZE THE USE IN THIS STATE OF A FICTITIOUS BUSINESS NAME IN VIOLATION OF THE RIGHTS OF ANOTHER UNDER FEDERAL, STATE, OR COMMON LAW (SEE SECTION 14400 ET SEQ. BUSINESS AND PROFESSIONS CODE).

CERTIFICATION
I HEREBY CERTIFY THAT THE FOREGOING IS A CORRECT COPY OF THE ORIGINAL ON FILE IN MY OFFICE.

FRANK S. ZOLIN,
COUNTY CLERK/EXECUTIVE OFFICER

BY_____ , DEPUTY

FILE NO._____

*Government forms may vary each year. Consult your current year's forms for complete information.

Form 8

Fictitious Business Name Statement (continued)

INSTRUCTIONS FOR COMPLETION OF STATE   (Please type or print in black ink)

(1)   At the top of the Statement, check "First Filing" if this is your initial registration. If this is a renewal filing because of the expiration of your current registration, check "Renewal Filing" and insert your current registration number.

(2)   Insert the fictitious business name or names if more than one name is being filed.

(3)   If the registrant has a place of business in this state, insert the street address of his principal place of business in this state. If the registrant has no place of business in this state, insert the street address of his principal place of business outside this state (P. O. Box not acceptable).

(4)   If the registrant is an individual, insert his full name and residence address. (P. O. Box not acceptable for residence address.)

        If the registrant is a partnership or other association of persons, insert the full name and residence address of each general partner.

        If the registrant is a corporation, they are required to submit either a certified copy of the Articles of Incorporation (a copy is acceptable), or an Affidavit signed under penalty of perjury by one of the Officers of the Corporation. Insert the name of the corporation as set forth in its Articles of Incorporation, the State of Incorporation, and the principal business address. (P. O. Box not acceptable.)

(5)   Check box provided, whichever of the following best describes the nature of the business:
        "an individual," "a general partnership," "a limited partnership," "an unincorporated association other than a partnership," "corporation," "business trust," "co-partners," "husband & wife," "joint venture," "other," as defined in (Sec. 17901, 17902, B&P Code).

(6)   Date business commenced.

(7)   Signature(s) of Registrants.

        If the registrant is an individual, the statement shall be signed by the individual.

        If the registrant is a partnership or other association of other persons, the statement shall be signed by a general partner.

        If the registrant is a business trust, the statement shall be signed by a trustee.

        If the registrants are co-partner, the statement shall be signed by ALL partners.

        If the registrants are husband and wife, the statement shall be signed by both. (Two Signatures Required.)

        If the registration is a joint venture, the statement shall be signed by all parties of the joint venture, NOTE: Attach a signature sheet if more than (2) parties.

(8)   If the registrant is a corporation, the statement shall be signed by an officer. State title of officer. Attach a copy of Articles of Incorporation.

NOTICE TO REGISTRANT PURSUANT TO SECTION 17924 BUSINESS & PROFESSIONS CODE

(A)   Your fictitious business name statement must be published in a newspaper within 30 days after the statement has been filed with the County Clerk. The statement must be published once a week for four successive weeks and an affidavit of publication filed with the County Clerk within 30 days after publication has been completed. If this is not completed within the time allowed the registration will be voided. (Or expires immediately.) The statement should be published in a newspaper of general circulation in the County where the principal place of business is located. The statement should be published in such County in a newspaper that circulates in the area where the business is to be conducted. (Sec. 17917, B&P Code).

(B)   Any person who executes, files or publishes any fictitious business name statement, knowing that such statement is false, in whole or in part is guilty of a misdemeanor and upon conviction thereof shall be fined not to exceed five hundred dollars ($500). (Sec. 17930, B&P Code).

EXPIRATIONS

A fictitious business name statement expires at the end of five years from the date it was filed with the County Clerk, and a new statement must be filed. The new statement need not be re-published if there has been NO change in the facts contained in the statement previously filed.

Except as provided in Section 17923 B&PC, a statement expires 40 days after ANY change in the facts contained in the statement EXCEPT that a change in the residence address of an individual does not cause it to expire.

A corporation is required to file a new statement after a change in its corporate name.

A statement expires when an abandonment has been filed.

PUBLICATION

If this is a new business name being filed refer to paragraph A above.

When a new statement is required because the current statement will expire at the end of 5 years from the date on which it was filed, the new statement NEED NOT be published UNLESS there has been a change in the information required in the prior statement. If publication is required refer to paragraph A above.

ES-F: wpc(v)
ASO #7 Inst:BF&R

---

*Government forms may vary each year. Consult your current year's forms for complete information.

Form 9

State Name Reservation

Date

Office of Secretary of State

Street

City, State, Zip

Dear Sir/Madam:

     I would like to reserve a proposed corporate name. The alternative name choices in order of preference are:
(1) _____, (2) _____, and (3) _____.
The principal business will be in [type of business] and the principal office shall be located in _____ County.

     I have enclosed a check in the amount of _____ dollars to cover the certification cost as required by law.

     If you have further questions, please call me.

Thank you.

Sincerely,

_____

Owner

Form 10

IRS Form SS-4: Federal Employer Identification Number with Instructions

Form **SS-4** Department of the Treasury Internal Revenue Service	**Application for Employer Identification Number** (For use by employers, corporations, partnerships, trusts, estates, churches, government agencies, certain individuals, and others. See instructions.)	EIN OMB No. 1545-0003

Please type or print clearly.

1 Name of applicant (Legal name) (See instructions.)

2 Trade name of business, if different from name in line 1	**3** Executor, trustee, "care of" name
4a Mailing address (street address) (room, apt., or suite no.)	**5a** Business address, if different from address in lines 4a and 4b
4b City, state, and ZIP code	**5b** City, state, and ZIP code

6 County and state where principal business is located

7 Name of principal officer, general partner, grantor, owner, or trustor—SSN required (See instructions.) ► _____

8a Type of entity (Check only one box.) (See instructions.)
- ☐ Sole Proprietor (SSN) _____
- ☐ REMIC
- ☐ State/local government ☐ National guard
- ☐ Other nonprofit organization (specify) _____
- ☐ Other (specify) ► _____
- ☐ Personal service corp.
- ☐ Estate (SSN of decedent) _____
- ☐ Plan administrator-SSN _____
- ☐ Other corporation (specify) _____
- ☐ Federal government/military ☐ Church or church controlled organization
- ☐ Trust
- ☐ Partnership
- ☐ Farmers' cooperative
(enter GEN if applicable) _____

8b If a corporation, name the state or foreign country (if applicable) where incorporated ►

State	Foreign country

9 Reason for applying (Check only one box.)
- ☐ Started new business (specify) ► _____
- ☐ Hired employees
- ☐ Created a pension plan (specify type) ► _____
- ☐ Banking purpose (specify) ►
- ☐ Changed type of organization (specify) ► _____
- ☐ Purchased going business
- ☐ Created a trust (specify) ► _____
- ☐ Other (specify) ►

10 Date business started or acquired (Mo., day, year) (See instructions.)	**11** Enter closing month of accounting year. (See instructions.)

12 First date wages or annuities were paid or will be paid (Mo., day, year). **Note:** If applicant is a withholding agent, enter date income will first be paid to nonresident alien. (Mo., day, year) . . . . ►

13 Enter highest number of employees expected in the next 12 months. **Note:** If the applicant does not expect to have any employees during the period, enter "0." . . . . ►

Nonagricultural	Agricultural	Household

14 Principal activity (See instructions.) ►

15 Is the principal business activity manufacturing? . . . . ☐ Yes ☐ No
If "Yes," principal product and raw material used ►

16 To whom are most of the products or services sold? Please check the appropriate box. ☐ Business (wholesale)
☐ Public (retail) ☐ Other (specify) ► ☐ N/A

17a Has the applicant ever applied for an identification number for this or any other business? . . . . ☐ Yes ☐ No
Note: If "Yes," please complete lines 17b and 17c.

17b If you checked the "Yes" box in line 17a, give applicant's legal name and trade name, if different than name shown on prior application.

Legal name ► Trade name ►

17c Enter approximate date, city, and state where the application was filed and the previous employer identification number if known.

Approximate date when filed (Mo., day, year)	City and state where filed	Previous EIN

Under penalties of perjury, I declare that I have examined this application, and to the best of my knowledge and belief, it is true, correct, and complete. | Business telephone number (include area code)

Name and title (Please type or print clearly.) ►

Signature ► Date ►

Note: Do not write below this line. For official use only.

Please leave blank ►	Geo.	Ind.	Class	Size	Reason for applying

For Paperwork Reduction Act Notice, see attached instructions. Cat. No. 16055N Form **SS-4**

*Government forms may vary each year. Consult your current year's forms for complete information.

Form 10

IRS Form SS-4: Federal Employer Identification Number with Instructions (continued)

General Instructions

(Section references are to the Internal Revenue Code unless otherwise noted.)

Purpose

Use Form SS-4 to apply for an employer identification number (EIN). An EIN is a nine-digit number (for example, 12-3456789) assigned to sole proprietors, corporations, partnerships, estates, trusts, and other entities for filing and reporting purposes. The information you provide on this form will establish your filing and reporting requirements.

Who Must File

You must file this form if you have not obtained an EIN before and

● You pay wages to one or more employees.

● You are required to have an EIN to use on any return, statement, or other document, even if you are not an employer.

● You are a withholding agent required to withhold taxes on income, other than wages, paid to a nonresident alien (individual, corporation, partnership, etc.). A withholding agent may be an agent, broker, fiduciary, manager, tenant, or spouse, and is required to file **Form 1042**, Annual Withholding Tax Return for U.S. Source Income of Foreign Persons.

● You file **Schedule C**, Profit or Loss From Business, or **Schedule F**, Profit or Loss From Farming, of **Form 1040**, U.S. Individual Income Tax Return, and have a Keogh plan or are required to file excise, employment, or alcohol, tobacco, or firearms returns.

The following must use EINs even if they do not have any employees:

● Trusts, except the following:

  1. Certain grantor-owned revocable trusts (see the Instructions for Form 1040).

  2. Individual Retirment Arrangement (IRA) trusts, unless the trust has to file **Form 990-T**, Exempt Organization Business Income Tax Return (See the Instructions for Form 990-T.)

● Estates

● Partnerships

● REMICS (real estate mortgage investment conduits) (See the instructions for **Form 1066**, U.S. Real Estate Mortgage Investment Conduit Income Tax Return.)

● Corporations

● Nonprofit organizations (churches, clubs, etc.)

● Farmers' cooperatives

● Plan administrators (A plan administrator is the person or group of persons specified as the administrator by the instrument under which the plan is operated.)

Note: *Household employers are not required to file Form SS-4 to get an EIN. An EIN may be assigned to you without filing Form SS-4 if your only employees are household employees (domestic workers) in your private home. To have an EIN assigned to you, write "NONE" in the space for the EIN on* **Form 942**, *Employer's Quarterly Tax Return for Household Employees, when you file it.*

When To Apply for A New EIN

New Business.—If you become the new owner of an existing business, **DO NOT** use the EIN of the former owner. If you already have an EIN, use that number. If you do not have an EIN, apply for one on this form. If you become the "owner" of a corporation by acquiring its stock, use the corporation's EIN.

Changes in Organization or Ownership.—If you already have an EIN, you may need to get a new one if either the organization or ownership of your business changes. If you incorporate a sole proprietorship or form a partnership, you must get a new EIN. However, **DO NOT** apply for a new EIN if you change only the name of your business.

File Only One Form SS-4.—File only one Form SS-4, regardless of the number of businesses operated or trade names under which a business operates. However, each corporation in an affiliated group must file a separate application.

EIN Applied For, But Not Received.—If you do not have an EIN by the time a return is due, write "Applied for" and the date you applied in the space shown for the number. **DO NOT** show your social security number as an EIN on returns.

If you do not have an EIN by the time a tax deposit is due, send your payment to the Internal Revenue service center for your filing area. (See **Where To Apply** below.) Make your check or money order payable to Internal Revenue Service and show your name (as shown on Form SS-4), address, kind of tax, period covered, and date you applied for an EIN.

For more information about EINs, see **Pub. 583**, Taxpayers Starting a Business and **Pub. 1635**, EINs Made Easy.

How To Apply

You can apply for an EIN either by mail or by telephone. You can get an EIN immediately by calling the Tele-TIN phone number for the service center for your state, or you can send the completed Form SS-4 directly to the service center to receive your EIN in the mail.

Application by Tele-TIN.—Under the Tele-TIN program, you can receive your EIN over the telephone and use it

immediately to file a return or make a payment. To receive an EIN by phone, complete Form SS-4, then call the Tele-TIN phone number listed for your state under **Where To Apply.** The person making the call must be authorized to sign the form (see **Signature block** on page 3).

An IRS representative will use the information from the Form SS-4 to establish your account and assign you an EIN. Write the number you are given on the upper right-hand corner of the form, sign and date it.

You should mail or FAX the signed SS-4 within 24 hours to the Tele-TIN Unit at the service center address for your state. The IRS representative will give you the FAX number. The FAX numbers are also listed in Pub. 1635.

Taxpayer representatives can receive their client's EIN by phone if they first send a facsimile (FAX) of a completed **Form 2848**, Power of Attorney and Declaration of Representative, or **Form 8821**, Tax Information Authorization, to the Tele-TIN unit. The Form 2848 or Form 8821 will be used solely to release the EIN to the representative authorized on the form.

Application by Mail.—Complete Form SS-4 at least 4 to 5 weeks before you will need an EIN. Sign and date the application and mail it to the service center address for your state. You will receive your EIN in the mail in approximately 4 weeks.

Where To Apply

The Tele-TIN phone numbers listed below will involve a long-distance charge to callers outside of the local calling area, and should be used only to apply for an EIN. THE NUMBERS MAY CHANGE WITHOUT NOTICE. Use 1-800-829-1040 to verify a number or to ask about an application by mail or other Federal tax matters.

If your principal business, office or agency, or legal residence in the case of an individual, is located in:	Call the Tele-TIN phone number shown or file with the Internal Revenue Service center at:
Florida, Georgia, South Carolina	Attn: Entity Control Atlanta, GA 39901 (404) 455-2360
New Jersey, New York City and counties of Nassau, Rockland, Suffolk, and Westchester	Attn: Entity Control Holtsville, NY 00501 (516) 447-4955
New York (all other counties), Connecticut, Maine, Massachusetts, New Hampshire, Rhode Island, Vermont	Attn: Entity Control Andover, MA 05501 (508) 474-9717
Illinois, Iowa, Minnesota, Missouri, Wisconsin	Attn: Entity Control Stop 57A 2306 E. Bannister Rd. Kansas City, MO 64131 (816) 926-5999
Delaware, District of Columbia, Maryland, Pennsylvania, Virginia	Attn: Entity Control Philadelphia, PA 19255 (215) 574-2400

Appendix

*Government forms may vary each year. Consult your current year's forms for complete information.

Form 10

IRS Form SS-4: Federal Employer Identification Number with Instructions (continued)

Indiana, Kentucky, Michigan, Ohio, West Virginia	Attn: Entity Control Cincinnati, OH 45999 (606) 292-5467
Kansas, New Mexico, Oklahoma, Texas	Attn: Entity Control Austin, TX 73301 (512) 462-7843
Alaska, Arizona, California (counties of Alpine, Amador, Butte, Calaveras, Colusa, Contra Costa, Del Norte, El Dorado, Glenn, Humboldt, Lake, Lassen, Marin, Mendocino, Modoc, Napa, Nevada, Placer, Plumas, Sacramento, San Joaquin, Shasta, Sierra, Siskiyou, Solano, Sonoma, Sutter, Tehama, Trinity, Yolo, and Yuba), Colorado, Idaho, Montana, Nebraska, Nevada, North Dakota, Oregon, South Dakota, Utah, Washington, Wyoming	Attn: Entity Control Mail Stop 6271-T P.O. Box 9950 Ogden, UT 84409 (801) 620-7645
California (all other counties), Hawaii	Attn: Entity Control Fresno, CA 93888 (209) 452-4010
Alabama, Arkansas, Louisiana, Mississippi, North Carolina, Tennessee	Attn: Entity Control Memphis, TN 37501 (901) 365-5970

If you have no legal residence, principal place of business, or principal office or agency in any state, file your form with the Internal Revenue Service Center, Philadelphia, PA 19255 or call (215) 574-2400.

Specific Instructions

The instructions that follow are for those items that are not self-explanatory. Enter N/A (nonapplicable) on the lines that do not apply.

Line 1.—Enter the legal name of the entity applying for the EIN exactly as it appears on the social security card, charter, or other applicable legal document.

Individuals.—Enter the first name, middle initial, and last name.

Trusts.—Enter the name of the trust.

Estate of a decedent.—Enter the name of the estate.

Partnerships.—Enter the legal name of the partnership as it appears in the partnership agreement.

Corporations.—Enter the corporate name as set forth in the corporation charter or other legal document creating it.

Plan administrators.—Enter the name of the plan administrator. A plan administrator who already has an EIN should use that number.

Line 2.—Enter the trade name of the business if different from the legal name. The trade name is the "doing business as" name.

Note: *Use the full legal name on line 1 on all tax returns filed for the entity. However, if you enter a trade name on line 2 and choose to use the trade name instead of the legal name, enter the trade name on all returns you file. To prevent processing delays and errors, always use either the legal name only or the trade name only on all tax returns.*

Line 3.—Trusts enter the name of the trustee. Estates enter the name of the executor, administrator, or other fiduciary. If the entity applying has a designated person to receive tax information, enter that person's name as the "care of" person. Print or type the first name, middle initial, and last name.

Line 7.—Enter the first name, middle initial, last name, and social security number (SSN) of a principal officer if the business is a corporation; of a general partner if a partnership; and of a grantor owner, or trustor if a trust.

Line 8a.—Check the box that best describes the type of entity applying for the EIN. If not specifically mentioned, check the "other" box and enter the type of entity. Do not enter N/A.

Sole proprietor.—Check this box if you file Schedule C or F (Form 1040) and have a Keogh plan, or are required to file excise, employment, or alcohol, tobacco, or firearms returns. Enter your SSN (social security number) in the space provided.

Plan administrator.—If the plan administrator is an individual, enter the plan administrator's SSN in the space provided.

Withholding agent.—If you are a withholding agent required to file Form 1042, check the "other" box and enter "withholding agent."

REMICs.—Check this box if the entity has elected to be treated as a real estate mortgage investment conduit (REMIC). See the Instructions for Form 1066 for more information.

Personal service corporations.—Check this box if the entity is a personal service corporation. An entity is a personal service corporation for a tax year only if:

• The principal activity of the entity during the testing period (prior tax year) for the tax year is the performance of personal services substantially by employee-owners.

• The employee-owners own 10 percent of the fair market value of the outstanding stock in the entity on the last day of the testing period.

Personal services include performance of services in such fields as health, law, accounting, consulting, etc. For more information about personal service corporations, see the Instructions to **Form 1120,** U.S. Corporation Income Tax Return, and **Pub. 542,** Tax Information on Corporations.

Other corporations.—This box is for any corporation other than a personal service corporation. If you check this box, enter the type of corporation (such as insurance company) in the space provided.

Other nonprofit organizations.—Check this box if the nonprofit organization is

other than a church or church-controlled organization and specify the type of nonprofit organization (for example, an educational organization.)

If the organization also seeks tax-exempt status, you must file either **Package 1023** or **Package 1024,** Application for Recognition of Exemption. Get Pub. 557, Tax-Exempt Status for Your Organization, for more information.

Group exemption number (GEN).—If the organization is covered by a group exemption letter, enter the four-digit GEN. (Do not confuse the GEN with the nine-digit EIN.) If you do not know the GEN, contact the parent organization. Get Pub. 557 for more information about group exemption numbers.

Line 9.—Check only **one** box. Do not enter N/A.

Started new business.—Check this box if you are starting a new business that requires an EIN. If you check this box, enter the type of business being started. **DO NOT** apply if you already have an EIN and are only adding another place of business.

Changed type of organization.—Check this box if the business is changing its type of organization, for example, if the business was a sole proprietorship and has been incorporated or has become a partnership. If you check this box, specify in the space provided the type of change made, for example, "from sole proprietorship to partnership."

Purchased going business.—Check this box if you purchased an existing business. DO NOT use the former owner's EIN. Use your own EIN if you already have one.

Hired employees.—Check this box if the existing business is requesting an EIN because it has hired or is hiring employees and is therefore required to file employment tax returns. **DO NOT** apply if you already have an EIN and are only hiring employees. If you are hiring household employees, see **Note** under **Who Must File** on page 2.

Created a trust.—Check this box if you created a trust, and enter the type of trust created.

Note: *DO NOT file this form if you are the individual-grantor/owner of a revocable trust. You must use your SSN for that trust. See the instructions for Form 1040.*

Created a pension plan.—Check this box if you have created a pension plan and need this number for reporting purposes. Also, enter the type of plan created.

Banking purpose.—Check this box if you are requesting an EIN for banking purposes only and enter the banking purpose (for example, a bowling league for depositing dues, an investment club for dividend and interest reporting, etc.).

---

*Government forms may vary each year. Consult your current year's forms for complete information.

Form 10

IRS Form SS-4: Federal Employer Identification Number with Instructions (continued)

Indiana, Kentucky, Michigan, Ohio, West Virginia	Attn: Entity Control Cincinnati, OH 45999 (606) 292-5467
Kansas, New Mexico, Oklahoma, Texas	Attn: Entity Control Austin, TX 73301 (512) 462-7843
Alaska, Arizona, California (counties of Alpine, Amador, Butte, Calaveras, Colusa, Contra Costa, Del Norte, El Dorado, Glenn, Humboldt, Lake, Lassen, Marin, Mendocino, Modoc, Napa, Nevada, Placer, Plumas, Sacramento, San Joaquin, Shasta, Sierra, Siskiyou, Solano, Sonoma, Sutter, Tehama, Trinity, Yolo, and Yuba), Colorado, Idaho, Montana, Nebraska, Nevada, North Dakota, Oregon, South Dakota, Utah, Washington, Wyoming	Attn: Entity Control Mail Stop 6271-T P.O. Box 9950 Ogden, UT 84409 (801) 620-7645
California (all other counties), Hawaii	Attn: Entity Control Fresno, CA 93888 (209) 452-4010
Alabama, Arkansas, Louisiana, Mississippi, North Carolina, Tennessee	Attn: Entity Control Memphis, TN 37501 (901) 365-5970

If you have no legal residence, principal place of business, or principal office or agency in any state, file your form with the Internal Revenue Service Center, Philadelphia, PA 19255 or call (215) 574-2400.

Specific Instructions

The instructions that follow are for those items that are not self-explanatory. Enter N/A (nonapplicable) on the lines that do not apply.

Line 1.—Enter the legal name of the entity applying for the EIN exactly as it appears on the social security card, charter, or other applicable legal document.

Individuals.—Enter the first name, middle initial, and last name.

Trusts.—Enter the name of the trust.

Estate of a decedent.—Enter the name of the estate.

Partnerships.—Enter the legal name of the partnership as it appears in the partnership agreement.

Corporations.—Enter the corporate name as set forth in the corporation charter or other legal document creating it.

Plan administrators.—Enter the name of the plan administrator. A plan administrator who already has an EIN should use that number.

Line 2.—Enter the trade name of the business if different from the legal name. The trade name is the "doing business as" name.

Note: *Use the full legal name on line 1 on all tax returns filed for the entity. However, if you enter a trade name on line 2 and choose to use the trade name instead of the legal name, enter the trade name on all returns you file. To prevent processing delays and errors, always use either the legal name only or the trade name only on all tax returns.*

Line 3.—Trusts enter the name of the trustee. Estates enter the name of the executor, administrator, or other fiduciary. If the entity applying has a designated person to receive tax information, enter that person's name as the "care of" person. Print or type the first name, middle initial, and last name.

Line 7.—Enter the first name, middle initial, last name, and social security number (SSN) of a principal officer if the business is a corporation; of a general partner if a partnership; and of a grantor owner, or trustor if a trust.

Line 8a.—Check the box that best describes the type of entity applying for the EIN. If not specifically mentioned, check the "other" box and enter the type of entity. Do not enter N/A.

Sole proprietor.—Check this box if you file Schedule C or F (Form 1040) and have a Keogh plan, or are required to file excise, employment, or alcohol, tobacco, or firearms returns. Enter your SSN (social security number) in the space provided.

Plan administrator.—If the plan administrator is an individual, enter the plan administrator's SSN in the space provided.

Withholding agent.—If you are a withholding agent required to file Form 1042, check the "other" box and enter "withholding agent."

REMICs.—Check this box if the entity has elected to be treated as a real estate mortgage investment conduit (REMIC). See the Instructions for Form 1066 for more information.

Personal service corporations.—Check this box if the entity is a personal service corporation. An entity is a personal service corporation for a tax year only if:

• The principal activity of the entity during the testing period (prior tax year) for the tax year is the performance of personal services substantially by employee-owners.

• The employee-owners own 10 percent of the fair market value of the outstanding stock in the entity on the last day of the testing period.

Personal services include performance of services in such fields as health, law, accounting, consulting, etc. For more information about personal service corporations, see the Instructions to **Form 1120**, U.S. Corporation Income Tax Return, and **Pub. 542**, Tax Information on Corporations.

Other corporations.—This box is for any corporation other than a personal service corporation. If you check this box, enter the type of corporation (such as insurance company) in the space provided.

Other nonprofit organizations.—Check this box if the nonprofit organization is

other than a church or church-controlled organization and specify the type of nonprofit organization (for example, an educational organization.)

If the organization also seeks tax-exempt status, you must file either **Package 1023 or Package 1024,** Application for Recognition of Exemption. Get **Pub. 557,** Tax-Exempt Status for Your Organization, for more information.

Group exemption number (GEN).—If the organization is covered by a group exemption letter, enter the four-digit GEN. (Do not confuse the GEN with the nine-digit EIN.) If you do not know the GEN, contact the parent organization. Get Pub. 557 for more information about group exemption numbers.

Line 9.—Check only **one** box. Do not enter N/A.

Started new business.—Check this box if you are starting a new business that requires an EIN. If you check this box, enter the type of business being started. **DO NOT** apply if you already have an EIN and are only adding another place of business.

Changed type of organization.—Check this box if the business is changing its type of organization, for example, if the business was a sole proprietorship and has been incorporated or has become a partnership. If you check this box, specify in the space provided the type of change made, for example, "from sole proprietorship to partnership."

Purchased going business.—Check this box if you purchased an existing business. DO NOT use the former owner's EIN. Use your own EIN if you already have one.

Hired employees.—Check this box if the existing business is requesting an EIN because it has hired or is hiring employees and is therefore required to file employment tax returns. **DO NOT** apply if you already have an EIN and are only hiring employees. If you are hiring household employees, see **Note** under **Who Must File** on page 2.

Created a trust.—Check this box if you created a trust, and enter the type of trust created.

Note: *DO NOT file this form if you are the individual-grantor/owner of a revocable trust. You must use your SSN for the trust. See the instructions for Form 1040.*

Created a pension plan.—Check this box if you have created a pension plan and need this number for reporting purposes. Also, enter the type of plan created.

Banking purpose.—Check this box if you are requesting an EIN for banking purposes only and enter the banking purpose (for example, a bowling league for depositing dues, an investment club for dividend and interest reporting, etc.).

*Government forms may vary each year. Consult your current year's forms for complete information.

178

Form 10

IRS Form SS-4: Federal Employer Identification Number with Instructions (continued)

Other (specify).—Check this box if you are requesting an EIN for any reason other than those for which there are checkboxes, and enter the reason.

Line 10.—If you are starting a new business, enter the starting date of the business. If the business you acquired is already operating, enter the date you acquired the business. Trusts should enter the date the trust was legally created. Estates should enter the date of death of the decedent whose name appears on line 1 or the date when the estate was legally funded.

Line 11.—Enter the last month of your accounting year or tax year. An accounting or tax year is usually 12 consecutive months, either a calendar year or a fiscal year (including a period of 52 or 53 weeks). A calendar year is 12 consecutive months ending on December 31. A fiscal year is either 12 consecutive months ending on the last day of any month other than December or a 52-53 week year. For more information on accounting periods, see **Pub. 538,** Accounting Periods and Methods.

Individuals.—Your tax year generally will be a calendar year.

Partnerships.—Partnerships generally must adopt the tax year of either (1) the majority partners; (2) the principal partners; (3) the tax year that results in the least aggregate (total) deferral of income; or (4) some other tax year. (See the Instructions for **Form 1065,** U.S. Partnership Return of Income, for more information.)

REMICs.—Remics must have a calendar year as their tax year.

Personal service corporations.—A personal service corporation generally must adopt a calendar year unless:

● It can establish a business purpose for having a different tax year, or

● It elects under section 444 to have a tax year other than a calendar year.

Trusts.—Generally, a trust must adopt a calendar year except for the following:

● Tax-exempt trusts,

● Charitable trusts, and

● Grantor-owned trusts.

Line 12.—If the business has or will have employees, enter the date on which the business began or will begin to pay wages. If the business does not plan to have employees, enter N/A.

Withholding agent.—Enter the date you began or will begin to pay income to a nonresident alien. This also applies to individuals who are required to file Form 1042 to report alimony paid to a nonresident alien.

Line 14.—Generally, enter the exact type of business being operated (for example, advertising agency, farm, food or beverage establishment, labor union, real estate agency, steam laundry, rental of coin-operated vending machine, investment club, etc.). Also state if the business will involve the sale or distribution of alcoholic beverages.

Governmental.—Enter the type of organization (state, county, school district, or municipality, etc.).

Nonprofit organization (other than governmental).—Enter whether organized for religious, educational, or humane purposes, and the principal activity (for example, religious organization—hospital, charitable).

Mining and quarrying.—Specify the process and the principal product (for example, mining bituminous coal, contract drilling for oil, quarrying dimension stone, etc.).

Contract construction.—Specify whether general contracting or special trade contracting. Also, show the type of work normally performed (for example, general contractor for residential buildings, electrical subcontractor, etc.).

Food or beverage establishments.—Specify the type of establishment and state whether you employ workers who receive tips (for example, lounge—yes).

Trade.—Specify the type of sales and the principal line of goods sold (for example, wholesale dairy products, manufacturer's representative for mining machinery, retail hardware, etc.).

Manufacturing.—Specify the type of establishment operated (for example, sawmill, vegetable cannery, etc.).

Signature block.—The application must be signed by: (1) the individual, if the applicant is an individual, (2) the president, vice president, or other principal officer, if the applicant is a corporation, (3) a responsible and duly authorized member or officer having knowledge of its affairs, if the applicant is a partnership or other unincorporated organization, or (4) the fiduciary, if the applicant is a trust or estate.

Some Useful Publications

You may get the following publications for additional information on the subjects covered on this form. To get these and other free forms and publications, call 1-800-TAX-FORM (1-800-829-3676).

Pub. 1635, EINs Made Easy

Pub. 538, Accounting Periods and Methods

Pub. 541, Tax Information on Partnerships

Pub. 542, Tax Information on Corporations

Pub. 557, Tax-Exempt Status for Your Organization

Pub. 583, Taxpayers Starting A Business

Pub. 937, Employment Taxes and Information Returns

Package 1023, Application for Recognition of Exemption

Package 1024, Application for Recognition of Exemption Under Section 501(a) or for Determination Under Section 120

Paperwork Reduction Act Notice

We ask for the information on this form to carry out the Internal Revenue laws of the United States. You are required to give us the information. We need it to ensure that you are complying with these laws and to allow us to figure and collect the right amount of tax.

The time needed to complete and file this form will vary depending on individual circumstances. The estimated average time is:

Recordkeeping . . . . . . 7 min.

Learning about the law or the form . . . . . . 18 min.

Preparing the form . . . . . 44 min.

Copying, assembling, and sending the form to the IRS . 20 min.

If you have comments concerning the accuracy of these time estimates or suggestions for making this form more simple, we would be happy to hear from you. You can write to both the **Internal Revenue Service,** Attention: Reports Clearance Officer, PC:FP, Washington, DC 20224; and the **Office of Management and Budget,** Paperwork Reduction Project (1545-0003), Washington, DC 20503. **DO NOT** send this form to either of these offices. Instead, see **Where To Apply** on page 2.

Printed on recycled paper

*Government forms may vary each year. Consult your current year's forms for complete information.

Form 11

IRS Form SS-8: Independent Contractor Factors

Form **SS-8** (Rev. January 1988) Department of the Treasury Internal Revenue Service	Information for Use in Determining Whether a Worker Is an Employee for Federal Employment Taxes and Income Tax Withholding	OMB No. 1545-0004

Paperwork Reduction Act Notice.—We ask for this information to carry out the Internal Revenue laws of the United States. We need it to ensure that taxpayers are complying with these laws and to allow us to figure and collect the right amount of tax. If you want a determination on employment status, you are required to give us this information.

Instructions

This form should be completed carefully. If the firm is completing the form, it should be completed for ONE individual who is representative of the class of workers whose status is in question.

If a written determination is desired for more than one class of workers, a separate Form SS-8 should be completed for one worker from each class whose status is typical of that class. A written determination for any worker will be applicable to other workers of the same class if the facts are not materially different from those of the worker whose status was ruled upon.

Please return Form SS-8 to the Internal Revenue Service office that provided the form. If the Internal Revenue Service did not ask you to complete this form but you wish a determination on whether a worker is an employee, file Form SS-8 with your District Director.

Name of firm (or person) for whom the worker performed services	Name of worker
Address of firm (include street address, city, state, and ZIP code)	Address of worker (include street address, city, state, and ZIP code)
Trade name	Telephone number	Worker's social security number
Telephone number	Firm's taxpayer identification number	

Check type of firm

☐ **Individual**   ☐ **Partnership**   ☐ **Corporation**   ☐ **Other** (specify) ▶

This form is being completed by   ☐ **FIRM** · ☐ **WORKER**

If the form is being completed by the worker, do you object to disclosing your name or the information on this form to the firm? . . . . ☐ **Yes** ☐ **No**

(If your answer is YES, we are not able to furnish you a determination on the basis of this form. You may write to your District Director for further information. **Do not complete the rest of the form, unless the IRS requests it.**)

All items must be answered or marked "Unknown" or "Not Applicable" (NA). If you need more space, attach another sheet. This form is designed to cover many work activities, so some of the questions may not pertain to you.

Total number of workers in this class (if more than one, please see item 19) ▶ _____

This information is about services performed by the worker from ▶ _____ to _____
(Month, day, year) (Month, day, year)

What was the first date on which the worker performed services of any kind for the firm? ▶ _____
(Month, day, year)

Is the worker still performing services for the firm? . . . . ☐ **Yes** ☐ **No**
If "No," what was the date of termination? ▶ _____
(Month, day, year)

In which IRS district are you located? _____

1a Describe the firm's business _____
_____
_____

b Describe the work done by the worker _____
_____
_____
_____

2a If the work is done under a written agreement between the firm and the worker, attach a copy.
b If the agreement is not in writing, describe the terms and conditions of the work arrangement _____
_____
_____
_____
_____

Form **SS-8**

---

*Government forms may vary each year. Consult your current year's forms for complete information.

Form 11

IRS Form SS-8: Independent Contractor Factors (continued)

c If the actual working arrangement differs in any way from the agreement, explain the differences and why they occur ....
....
....

3a Is the worker given training by the firm? . . . . ☐ Yes   ☐ No
     If yes:
         What kind? ....
         How often? ....
b Is the worker given instructions in the way the work is to be done? . . . . ☐ Yes   ☐ No
     If yes, give specific examples. ....
c Attach representative copies of any written instructions or procedures.
d Does the firm have the right to change the methods used by the worker or direct that person on how to do the work? ☐ Yes   ☐ No
     Explain your answer ....
....
e Does the operation of the firm's business require that the worker be supervised or controlled in the performance of
     the service? . . . . ☐ Yes   ☐ No
     Explain your answer ....
....

4a The firm engages the worker:
     ☐ To perform and complete a particular job only.
     ☐ To work at a job for an indefinite period of time.
     ☐ Other (explain) ....
b Is the worker required to follow a routine or a schedule established by the firm? . . . . ☐ Yes   ☐ No
     If yes, what is the routine or schedule? ....
....

c Does the worker report to the firm or its representative? . . . . ☐ Yes   ☐ No
     If yes:
         How often? ....
         For what purpose? ....
         In what manner (in person, in writing, by telephone, etc.)? ....
         Attach copies of report forms used in reporting to the firm.
d Does the worker furnish a time record to the firm? . . . . ☐ Yes   ☐ No
     If yes, attach copies of time records.
5a State the kind and value of tools and equipment furnished by:
     The firm ....
....
     The worker ....
....
b State the kind and value of supplies and materials furnished by:
     The firm ....
....
     The worker ....
....
c What expenses are incurred by the worker in the performance of services for the firm?
....
d Does the firm reimburse the worker for any expenses? . . . . ☐ Yes   ☐ No
     If yes, specify the reimbursed expenses ....

6a Is it understood that the worker will perform the services personally? . . . . ☐ Yes   ☐ No
b Does the worker have helpers? . . . . ☐ Yes   ☐ No
     If yes: Are the helpers hired by: ☐ Firm   ☐ Worker
     If hired by the worker, is the firm's approval necessary? . . . . ☐ Yes   ☐ No
     Who pays the helpers? ☐ Firm   ☐ Worker
     Are social security taxes and Federal income tax withheld from the helpers' wages? . . . . ☐ Yes   ☐ No
     If yes: Who reports and pays these taxes? ☐ Firm   ☐ Worker
     Who reports the helpers' incomes to the Internal Revenue Service? ☐ Firm   ☐ Worker
     If the worker pays the helpers, does the firm repay the worker? . . . . ☐ Yes   ☐ No
     What services do the helpers perform? ....

*Government forms may vary each year. Consult your current year's forms for complete information.

Form 11

IRS Form SS-8: Independent Contractor Factors (continued)

Form SS-8

Page **3**

7 At what location are the services performed? ☐ Firm's ☐ Worker's ☐ Other (specify) ....

8a Type of pay worker receives:
☐ Salary ☐ Commission ☐ Hourly wage ☐ Piecework ☐ Lump sum ☐ Other (specify)...............

b Does the firm guarantee a minimum amount of pay to the worker? . . . . ☐ Yes ☐ No

c Does the firm allow the worker a drawing account or advances against pay?. . . . . ☐ Yes ☐ No
If yes: Is the worker paid such advances on a regular basis?. ☐ Yes ☐ No
How does the worker repay such advances?

9a Is the worker eligible for a pension, bonuses, paid vacations, sick pay, etc.?. . . . . ☐ Yes ☐ No
If yes specify ....

b Does the firm carry workmen's compensation insurance on the worker? . . . . ☐ Yes ☐ No

c Does the firm deduct social security tax from amounts paid the worker? . . . . ☐ Yes ☐ No

d Does the firm deduct Federal income taxes from amounts paid the worker? . . . . ☐ Yes ☐ No

e How does the firm report the worker's income to the Internal Revenue Service?
☐ Form W-2 ☐ Form 1099 ☐ Does not report ☐ Other (specify) ....

f Does the firm bond the worker?. . . . . ☐ Yes ☐ No

10a Approximately how many hours a day does the worker perform services for the firm? ....

b Does the worker perform similar services for others? . . . . ☐ Yes ☐ No ☐ Unknown
If yes: Are these services performed on a daily basis for other firms? . . . . ☐ Yes ☐ No ☐ Unknown
Percentage of time spent in performing these services for:
This firm ....% Other firms...........% ☐ Unknown
Does the firm have priority on the worker's time? . . . . ☐ Yes ☐ No
If no, explain...

c Is the worker prohibited from competing with the firm either while performing services or during any later period? . . ☐ Yes ☐ No

11a Can the firm discharge the worker at any time without incurring a liability? . . . . ☐ Yes ☐ No
If no, explain..

b Can the worker terminate the services at any time without incurring a liability? . . . . ☐ Yes ☐ No
If no, explain..

12a Does the worker perform services for the firm under:
☐ The firm's business name ☐ The worker's own business name ☐ Other (specify) ....

b Does the worker advertise or maintain a business listing in the telephone directory, a trade journal, etc.? ☐ Yes ☐ No ☐ Unknown
If yes, specify ....

c Does the worker represent himself or herself to the public as being in business to perform the
same or similar services? . . . . ☐ Yes ☐ No ☐ Unknown
If yes, how?..

d Does the worker have his or her own shop or office? . . . . ☐ Yes ☐ No ☐ Unknown
If yes, where?...

e Does the firm represent the worker as an employee of the firm to its customers? . . . . ☐ Yes ☐ No
If no, how is the worker represented? ....

f How did the firm learn of the worker's services? ....

13 Is a license necessary for the work? . . . . ☐ Yes ☐ No ☐ Unknown
If yes, what kind of license is required?...............................
By whom is it issued? ....
By whom is the license fee paid?......................................

14 Does the worker have a financial investment in a business related to the services performed? . . . . ☐ Yes ☐ No ☐ Unknown
If yes, specify and give amounts of the investment ....

15 Can the worker incur a loss in the performance of the service for the firm? . . . . ☐ Yes ☐ No
If yes, how?...

16a Has any other government agency ruled on the status of the firm's workers? . . . . ☐ Yes ☐ No
If yes, attach a copy of the ruling.

b Is the same issue being considered by any IRS office in connection with the audit of the worker's tax return or the
firm's tax return, or has it recently been considered? . . . . ☐ Yes ☐ No
If yes, for which year(s)? ....

17 Does the worker assemble or process a product at home or away from the firm's place of business?. . . . . . . ☐ Yes ☐ No
If yes:
Who furnishes materials or goods used by the worker? ☐ Firm ☐ Worker
Is the worker furnished a pattern or given instructions to follow in making the product? . . . . ☐ Yes ☐ No
Is the worker required to return the finished product to the firm or to someone designated by the firm? . . . . ☐ Yes ☐ No

*Government forms may vary each year. Consult your current year's forms for complete information.

Form 11

IRS Form SS-8: Independent Contractor Factors (continued)

Answer items 18a through n if the worker is a salesman or provides a service directly to customers.

18a Are leads to prospective customers furnished by the firm? . . . . ☐ Yes ☐ No ☐ **Does not apply**

  b Is the worker required to pursue or report on leads? . . . . ☐ Yes ☐ No ☐ **Does not apply**

  c Is the worker required to adhere to prices, terms, and conditions of sale established by the firm? . . . . ☐ Yes ☐ No

  d Are orders submitted to and subject to approval by the firm? . . . . ☐ Yes ☐ No

  e Is the worker expected to attend sales meetings? . . . . ☐ Yes ☐ No

    If yes: Is the worker subject to any kind of penalty for failing to attend? . . . . ☐ Yes ☐ No

  f Does the firm assign a specific territory to the worker? . . . . ☐ Yes ☐ No ☐ **Does not apply**

  g Who does the customer pay? ☐ Firm ☐ Worker

    If worker, does the worker remit the total amount to the firm?. . . . . ☐ Yes ☐ No

  h Does the worker sell a consumer product in a home or establishment other than a permanent retail establishment? . ☐ Yes ☐ No

  i List the products and/or services distributed by the worker, such as meat, vegetables, fruit, bakery products, beverages (other than milk), or laundry or dry cleaning services. If more than one type of product and/or service is distributed, specify the principal one. _____

  j Were the route or territory and a list of customers assigned to the worker by the firm or another person? . . . . . ☐ Yes ☐ No

    If yes, please identify the person who made the assignment. _____

  k Did the worker pay the firm or person for the privilege of serving customers on the route or in the territory? . . . . ☐ Yes ☐ No

    If yes, how much did the worker pay (not including any amount paid for a truck or racks, etc.)? $ _____

    What factors were considered in determining the value of the route or territory? _____

  l How are new customers obtained by the worker? Explain fully, showing whether the new customers called the firm for service, were solicited by the worker, or both. _____

  m Does the worker sell life insurance? . . . . ☐ Yes ☐ No

    If yes:

    Is the selling of life insurance or annuity contracts for the firm the worker's entire business activity? . . . . . ☐ Yes ☐ No

    If no, state the extent of the worker's other business activities _____

    Does the worker sell other types of insurance for the firm? . . . . ☐ Yes ☐ No

    If yes, state the percentage of the worker's total working time spent in selling such other types of insurance _____ %

    State if, at the time the contract was entered into between the firm and the worker, their intention was that the worker would be considered as selling life insurance for the firm (a) on a full-time basis, or (b) on a part-time basis. State the manner in which such intention was expressed. _____

  n Is the worker a traveling salesperson or city salesperson? . . . . ☐ Yes ☐ No

    If yes:

    Specify from whom the worker principally solicits orders on behalf of the firm. _____

    If the worker solicits orders from wholesalers, retailers, contractors, or operators of hotels, restaurants, or other similar establishments, specify the percentage of the worker's time spent in such solicitation. _____ %

    Is the merchandise purchased by the customers for resale, or is it purchased for use in their business operations? If used by the customers in their business operations, describe the merchandise and state whether it is equipment that is installed on their premises or is a consumable supply. _____

19 Attach the names and addresses of the total number of workers in this class from page 1, or the names and addresses of 10 such workers if there are more than 10.

20 Attach a detailed explanation for any other reason why you believe the worker is an independent contractor or is an employee of the firm.

IMPORTANT INFORMATION NEEDED TO PROCESS YOUR REQUEST

Under section 6110 of the Internal Revenue Code, the text and related background file documents of any ruling, determination letter, or technical advice memorandum will be open to public inspection. This section provides that before the text and background file documents are made public, identifying and certain other information must be deleted.

Are the names, addresses, and taxpayer identifying numbers the only items you want deleted? . . . . ☐ Yes ☐ No

If you checked No and believe additional deletions should be made, we cannot process your request unless you submit a copy of this form and copies of all supporting documents indicating, in brackets, those parts you believe should be deleted in accordance with section 6110(c) of the Code. Attach a separate statement indicating which specific exemption provided by section 6110(c) applies to each bracketed part.

Under penalties of perjury, I declare that I have examined this request, including accompanying documents, and to the best of my knowledge and belief, the facts presented are true, correct, and complete.

Signature ▶	Title ▶	Date ▶

If this form is used by the firm in requesting a written determination, the form should be signed by an officer or member of the firm.
If this form is used by the worker in requesting a written determination, the form should be signed by the worker. If the worker wants a written determination with respect to services performed for two or more firms, a separate form should be furnished for each firm.
Additional copies of this form may be obtained from any Internal Revenue Service office.

☆ U.S. Government Printing Office: 1988—201-993/60206

*Government forms may vary each year. Consult your current year's forms for complete information.

Form 12

IRS Form W-4

19 Form W-4   Department of the Treasury
Internal Revenue Service

Purpose. Complete Form W-4 so that your employer can withhold the correct amount of Federal income tax from your pay.

Exemption From Withholding. Read line 7 of the certificate below to see if you can claim exempt status. *If exempt, complete line 7; but do not complete lines 5 and 6.* No Federal income tax will be withheld from your pay. Your exemption is good for one year only. It expires February 15, 1993.

Basic Instructions. Employees who are not exempt should complete the Personal Allowances Worksheet. Additional worksheets are provided on page 2 for employees to adjust their withholding allowances based on itemized deductions, adjustments to income, or two-earner/two-job situations. Complete all worksheets that apply to your situation. The worksheets will help you figure

the number of withholding allowances you are entitled to claim. However, you may claim fewer allowances than this.

Head of Household. Generally, you may claim head of household filing status on your tax return only if you are unmarried and pay more than 50% of the costs of keeping up a home for yourself and your dependent(s) or other qualifying individuals.

Nonwage Income. If you have a large amount of nonwage income, such as interest or dividends, you should consider making estimated tax payments using Form 1040-ES. Otherwise, you may find that you owe additional tax at the end of the year.

Two-Earner/Two-Jobs. If you have a working spouse or more than one job, figure the total number of allowances you are entitled to claim on all jobs using worksheets from only one Form

W-4. This total should be divided among all jobs. Your withholding will usually be most accurate when all allowances are claimed on the W-4 filed for the highest paying job and zero allowances are claimed for the others.

Advance Earned Income Credit. If you are eligible for this credit, you can receive it added to your paycheck throughout the year. For details, get Form W-5 from your employer.

Check Your Withholding. After your W-4 takes effect, you can use Pub. 919, Is My Withholding Correct for 1992?, to see how the dollar amount you are having withheld compares to your estimated total annual tax. Call 1-800-829-3676 to order this publication. Check your local telephone directory for the IRS assistance number if you need further help.

Personal Allowances Worksheet   For 1992, the value of your personal exemption(s) is reduced if your income is over $105,250 ($157,900 if married filing jointly, $131,550 if head of household, or $78,950 if married filing separately). Get Pub. 919 for details.

A Enter "1" for yourself if no one else can claim you as a dependent . . . . A ____

B Enter "1" if: • You are single and have only one job; or
  • You are married, have only one job, and your spouse does not work; or
  • Your wages from a second job or your spouse's wages (or the total of both) are $1,000 or less. . . B ____

C Enter "1" for your spouse. But, you may choose to enter -0- if you are married and have either a working spouse or more than one job (this may help you avoid having too little tax withheld) . . . . C ____

D Enter number of dependents (other than your spouse or yourself) whom you will claim on your tax return . . . . D ____

E Enter "1" if you will file as head of household on your tax return (see conditions under "Head of Household," above) . E ____

F Enter "1" if you have at least $1,500 of child or dependent care expenses for which you plan to claim a credit . . F ____

G Add lines A through F and enter total here. *Note: This amount may be different from the number of exemptions you claim on your return* ▶ G ____

For accuracy, do all worksheets that apply.

• If you plan to itemize or claim adjustments to income and want to reduce your withholding, see the Deductions and Adjustments Worksheet on page 2.

• If you are single and have more than one job and your combined earnings from all jobs exceed $29,000 OR if you are married and have a working spouse or more than one job, and the combined earnings from all jobs exceed $50,000, see the Two-Earner/Two-Job Worksheet on page 2 If you want to avoid having too little tax withheld.

• If neither of the above situations applies, stop here and enter the number from line G on line 5 of Form W-4 below.

------------ Cut here and give the certificate to your employer. Keep the top portion for your records. ------------

Form W-4   **Employee's Withholding Allowance Certificate**   OMB No. 1545-0010

Department of the Treasury
Internal Revenue Service   ▶ For Privacy Act and Paperwork Reduction Act Notice, see reverse.   **19**

1 Type or print your first name and middle initial	Last name	2 Your social security number

Home address (number and street or rural route)

3 ☐ Single ☐ Married ☐ Married, but withhold at higher Single rate.
Note: *If married, but legally separated, or spouse is a nonresident alien, check the Single box.*

City or town, state, and ZIP code

4 If your last name differs from that on your social security card, check here and call 1-800-772-1213 for more information . ▶ ☐

5 Total number of allowances you are claiming (from line G above or from the Worksheets on back if they apply)   **5** ____

6 Additional amount, if any, you want deducted from each paycheck . . . .   **6** $ ____

7 I claim exemption from withholding and I certify that I meet ALL of the following conditions for exemption:
• Last year I had a right to a refund of ALL Federal income tax withheld because I had NO tax liability; AND
• This year I expect a refund of ALL Federal income tax withheld because I expect to have NO tax liability; AND
• This year if my income exceeds $600 and includes nonwage income, another person cannot claim me as a dependent.
If you meet all of the above conditions, enter the year effective and "EXEMPT" here . . . ▶ **7** 19 ____

8 Are you a full-time student? (Note: *Full-time students are not automatically exempt.*) . . . . . . ▶   **8** ☐ Yes ☐ No

Under penalties of perjury, I certify that I am entitled to the number of withholding allowances claimed on this certificate or entitled to claim exempt status.

Employee's signature ▶ _____   Date ▶ _____ , 19 ___

9 Employer's name and address (Employer: Complete 9 and 11 only if sending to the IRS) | 10 Office code (optional) | 11 Employer identification number

---

*Government forms may vary each year. Consult your current year's forms for complete information.

Form 12

IRS Form W-4 (continued)

Deductions and Adjustments Worksheet

Note: *Use this worksheet only if you plan to itemize deductions or claim adjustments to income on your 1992 tax return.*

1. Enter an estimate of your 1992 itemized deductions. These include: qualifying home mortgage interest, charitable contributions, state and local taxes (but not sales taxes), medical expenses in excess of 7.5% of your income, and miscellaneous deductions. (For 1992, you may have to reduce your itemized deductions if your income is over $105,250 ($52,625 if married filing separately). Get Pub. 919 for details.)   **1** $ _____

2. Enter: { $6,000 if married filing jointly or qualifying widow(er)
   $5,250 if head of household
   $3,600 if single
   $3,000 if married filing separately }   **2** $ _____

3. Subtract line 2 from line 1. If line 2 is greater than line 1, enter -0-   **3** $ _____

4. Enter an estimate of your 1992 adjustments to income. These include alimony paid and deductible IRA contributions   **4** $ _____

5. Add lines 3 and 4 and enter the total   **5** $ _____

6. Enter an estimate of your 1992 nonwage income (such as dividends or interest income)   **6** $ _____

7. Subtract line 6 from line 5. Enter the result, but not less than -0-   **7** $ _____

8. Divide the amount on line 7 by $2,500 and enter the result here. Drop any fraction   **8**   _____

9. Enter the number from Personal Allowances Worksheet, line G, on page 1   **9**   _____

10. Add lines 8 and 9 and enter the total here. If you plan to use the Two-Earner/Two-Job Worksheet, also enter the total on line 1, below. Otherwise, stop here and enter this total on Form W-4, line 5, on page 1   **10**   _____

Two-Earner/Two-Job Worksheet

Note: *Use this worksheet only if the instructions for line G on page 1 direct you here.*

1. Enter the number from line G on page 1 (or from line 10 above if you used the Deductions and Adjustments Worksheet)   **1**   _____

2. Find the number in Table 1 below that applies to the LOWEST paying job and enter it here   **2**   _____

3. If line 1 is GREATER THAN OR EQUAL TO line 2, subtract line 2 from line 1. Enter the result here (if zero, enter -0-) and on Form W-4, line 5, on page 1. DO NOT use the rest of this worksheet   **3**   _____

Note: *If line 1 is LESS THAN line 2, enter -0- on Form W-4, line 5, on page 1. Complete lines 4–9 to calculate the additional dollar withholding necessary to avoid a year-end tax bill.*

4. Enter the number from line 2 of this worksheet   **4**   _____

5. Enter the number from line 1 of this worksheet   **5**   _____

6. Subtract line 5 from line 4   **6**   _____

7. Find the amount in Table 2 below that applies to the HIGHEST paying job and enter it here   **7** $ _____

8. Multiply line 7 by line 6 and enter the result here. This is the additional annual withholding amount needed   **8** $ _____

9. Divide line 8 by the number of pay periods remaining in 1992. (For example, divide by 26 if you are paid every other week and you complete this form in December of 1991.) Enter the result here and on Form W-4, line 6, page 1. This is the additional amount to be withheld from each paycheck   **9** $ _____

Table 1: Two-Earner/Two-Job Worksheet

Married Filing Jointly		All Others	
If wages from LOWEST paying job are—	Enter on line 2 above	If wages from LOWEST paying job are—	Enter on line 2 above
0 - $4,000	0	0 - $6,000	0
4,001 - 8,000	1	6,001 - 10,000	1
8,001 - 13,000	2	10,001 - 14,000	2
13,001 - 18,000	3	14,001 - 18,000	3
18,001 - 22,000	4	18,001 - 22,000	4
22,001 - 26,000	5	22,001 - 45,000	5
26,001 - 30,000	6	45,001 and over	6
30,001 - 35,000	7		
35,001 - 40,000	8		
40,001 - 60,000	9		
60,001 - 80,000	10		
80,001 and over	11		

Table 2: Two-Earner/Two-Job Worksheet

Married Filing Jointly		All Others	
If wages from HIGHEST paying job are—	Enter on line 7 above	If wages from HIGHEST paying job are—	Enter on line 7 above
0 - $50,000	$340	0 - $27,000	$340
50,001 - 100,000	640	27,001 - 58,000	640
100,001 and over	710	58,001 and over	710

Government forms may vary each year. Consult your current year's forms for complete information.

Form 13

INS Form I-9: Employment Eligibility Verification

U.S. Department of Justice
Immigration and Naturalization Service

OMB No. 1115-0136
Employment Eligibility Verification

Please read instructions carefully before completing this form. The instructions must be available during completion of this form. **ANTI-DISCRIMINATION NOTICE.** It is illegal to discriminate against work eligible individuals. Employers CANNOT specify which document(s) they will accept from an employee. The refusal to hire an individual because of a future expiration date may also constitute illegal discrimination.

Section 1. Employee Information and Verification. To be completed and signed by employee at the time employment begins

Print Name: Last	First	Middle Initial	Maiden Name
Address (Street Name and Number)		Apt. #	Date of Birth (month/day/year)
City	State	Zip Code	Social Security #

I am aware that federal law provides for imprisonment and/or fines for false statements or use of false documents in connection with the completion of this form.

I attest, under penalty of perjury, that I am (check one of the following):
☐ A citizen or national of the United States
☐ A Lawful Permanent Resident (Alien # A
☐ An alien authorized to work until ____/____/____
    (Alien # or Admission #

Employee's Signature

Date (month/day/year)

Preparer and/or Translator Certification. (To be completed and signed if Section 1 is prepared by a person other than the employee.) I attest, under penalty of perjury, that I have assisted in the completion of this form and that to the best of my knowledge the information is true and correct.

Preparer's/Translator's Signature	Print Name
Address (Street Name and Number, City, State, Zip Code)	Date (month/day/year)

Section 2. Employer Review and Verification. To be completed and signed by employer. Examine one document from List A OR examine one document from List B **and** one from List C as listed on the reverse of this form and record the title, number and expiration date, if any, of the document(s)

List A	OR	List B	AND	List C
Document title: _____		_____		_____
Issuing authority: _____		_____		_____
Document #: _____		_____		_____
Expiration Date (if any): __/__/__		__/__/__		__/__/__
Document #: _____				
Expiration Date (if any): __/__/__				

CERTIFICATION - I attest, under penalty of perjury, that I have examined the document(s) presented by the above-named employee, that the above-listed document(s) appear to be genuine and to relate to the employee named, that the employee began employment on (month/day/year) ____/____/____ and that to the best of my knowledge the employee is eligible to work in the United States. (State employment agencies may omit the date the employee began employment).

Signature of Employer or Authorized Representative	Print Name	Title
Business or Organization Name	Address (Street Name and Number, City, State, Zip Code)	Date (month/day/year)

Section 3. Updating and Reverification. To be completed and signed by employer

A. New Name (if applicable)	B. Date of rehire (month/day/year) (if applicable)

C. If employee's previous grant of work authorization has expired, provide the information below for the document that establishes current employment eligibility.

Document Title: _____ Document #: _____ Expiration Date (if any): ____/____/____

I attest, under penalty of perjury, that to the best of my knowledge, this employee is eligible to work in the United States, and if the employee presented document(s), the document(s) I examined appear to be genuine and to relate to the individual.

Signature of Employer or Authorized Representative	Date (month/day/year)

Form I-9

Appendix

*Government forms may vary each year. Consult your current year's forms for complete information.

Form 13

INS Form I-9: Employment Eligibility Verification (continued)

LISTS OF ACCEPTABLE DOCUMENTS

LIST A		LIST B		LIST C
Documents that Establish Both Identity and Employment Eligibility	OR	Documents that Establish Identity	AND	Documents that Establish Employment Eligibility

LIST A — Documents that Establish Both Identity and Employment Eligibility

1. U.S. Passport (unexpired or expired)

2. Certificate of U.S. Citizenship (INS Form N-560 or N-561)

3. Certificate of Naturalization (INS Form N-550 or N-570)

4. Unexpired foreign passport, with I-551 stamp or attached INS Form I-94 indicating unexpired employment authorization

5. Alien Registration Receipt Card with photograph (INS Form I-151 or I-551)

6. Unexpired Temporary Resident Card (INS Form I-688)

7. Unexpired Employment Authorization Card (INS Form I-688A)

8. Unexpired Reentry Permit (INS Form I-327)

9. Unexpired Refugee Travel Document (INS Form I-571)

10. Unexpired Employment Authorization Document issued by the INS which contains a photograph (INS Form I-688B)

LIST B — Documents that Establish Identity

1. Driver's license or ID card issued by a state or outlying possession of the United States provided it contains a photograph or information such as name, date of birth, sex, height, eye color, and address

2. ID card issued by federal, state, or local government agencies or entities provided it contains a photograph or information such as name, date of birth, sex, height, eye color, and address

3. School ID card with a photograph

4. Voter's registration card

5. U.S. Military card or draft record

6. Military dependent's ID card

7. U.S. Coast Guard Merchant Mariner Card

8. Native American tribal document

9. Driver's license issued by a Canadian government authority

For persons under age 18 who are unable to present a document listed above:

10. School record or report card

11. Clinic, doctor, or hospital record

12. Day-care or nursery school record

LIST C — Documents that Establish Employment Eligibility

1. U.S. social security card issued by the Social Security Administration (other than a card stating it is not valid for employment)

2. Certification of Birth Abroad issued by the Department of State (Form FS-545 or Form DS-1350)

3. Original or certified copy of a birth certificate issued by a state, county, municipal authority or outlying possession of the United States bearing an official seal

4. Native American tribal document

5. U.S. Citizen ID Card (INS Form I-197)

6. ID Card for use of Resident Citizen in the United States (INS Form I-179)

7. Unexpired employment authorization document issued by the INS (other than those listed under List A)

Illustrations of many of these documents appear in Part 8 of the Handbook for Employers (M-274)

Form I-9

*Government forms may vary each year. Consult your current year's forms for complete information.

Index

Appendix